ARCHITECTURAL DESIGN

GUEST-EDITED BY
MARJAN COLLETTI

EXUBERANCE
NEW VIRTUOSITY
IN CONTEMPORARY
ARCHITECTURE

02|2010

ARCHITECTURAL DESIGN
VOL 80, NO 2
MARCH/APRIL 2010
ISSN 0003-8504

PROFILE NO 204
ISBN 978-0470-717141

wiley.com

ARCHITECTURAL DESIGN

GUEST-EDITED BY
MARJAN COLLETTI

EXUBERANCE: NEW VIRTUOSITY IN CONTEMPORARY ARCHITECTURE

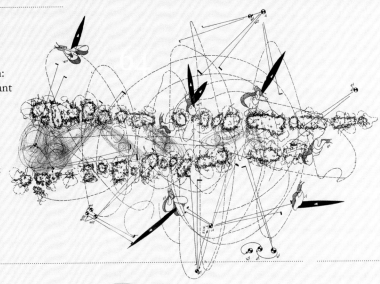

88

ARCHITECTURAL DESIGN
MARCH/APRIL 2010
PROFILE NO 204

Editorial Offices
John Wiley & Sons
25 John Street
London
WC1 N2BS

T: +44 (0)20 8326 3800

Editor
Helen Castle

Freelance Managing Editor
Caroline Ellerby

Production Editor
Elizabeth Gongde

Design and Prepress
Artmedia, London

Art Direction and Design
CHK Design:
Christian Küsters
Hannah Dumphy

Printed in Italy by Conti Tipocolor

Sponsorship/advertising
Faith Pidduck/Wayne Frost
T: +44 (0)1243 770254
E: fpidduck@wiley.co.uk

Subscribe to AD

AD is published bimonthly and is
available to purchase on both a
subscription basis and as individual
volumes at the following prices.

Prices
Individual copies: £22.99/$45.00
Mailing fees may apply

Annual Subscription Rates
Student: UK£70/US$110 print only
Individual: UK £110/US$170 print only
Institutional: UK£180/US$335
print or online
Institutional: UK£198/US$369
combined print and online

Subscription Offices UK
John Wiley & Sons Ltd
Journals Administration Department
1 Oldlands Way, Bognor Regis
West Sussex, PO22 9SA
T: +44 (0)1243 843272
F: +44 (0)1243 843232
E: cs-journals@wiley.co.uk

[ISSN: 0003-8504]

Prices are for six issues and include
postage and handling charges.
Periodicals postage paid at Jamaica,
NY 11431. Air freight and mailing in
the USA by Publications Expediting
Services Inc, 200 Meacham Avenue,
Elmont, NY 11003.
Individual rate subscriptions must be
paid by personal cheque or credit card.
Individual rate subscriptions may not
be resold or used as library copies.

All prices are subject to change
without notice.

Postmaster
Send address changes to Publications
Expediting Services Inc,
200 Meacham Avenue,
Elmont, NY 11003

Rights and Permissions
Requests to the Publisher should
be addressed to:
Permissions Department
John Wiley & Sons Ltd
The Atrium
Southern Gate
Chichester
West Sussex PO19 8SQ
England

F: +44 (0)1243 770620
E: permreq@wiley.co.uk

EDITORIAL
Helen Castle

It is entirely fitting that in 2010, in the year of our 80th anniversary (*AD* was founded in a basement in Bloomsbury in 1930), we should launch the redesign of *AD* with the *Exuberance* issue. Not only because the word 'exuberance' reflects our general excitement, enthusiasm, energy and high spirits, but also because the richness of its contents suggests much that has been strong, unique and potent about *AD*. This title, so adeptly guest-edited by Marjan Colletti, is highly visual. At a time when many architectural journals have taken a knocking in the current economic climate, *AD* remains one of the most image-rich publications, in recognition that architecture needs to communicate visually as well as verbally. It is printed in Italy to a high standard and illustrated throughout with high-quality colour images undisrupted by advertising. With the redesign, the art director, Christian Küsters of CHK Design, and the designer, Andrea Bettella of Artmedia, have put a great deal of effort into both ensuring continuity of style throughout the journal while maintaining the discrete identity of each article. The intention is to have a design that is both elegant and distinct, which gives space to the images: so that the images can both illustrate and enrich the meaning of the text, creating effectively a truly integrated page design.

Exuberance celebrates the aesthetics of architecture. This to some degree addresses the recent emphasis that has been placed on techniques and technologies in architecture. For here, most notably in the work of Colletti himself, Ali Rahim, Hernan Diaz Alonso and Tom Wiscombe, the formal overlays become integral to the digital. There is an understanding that architecture can become nuanced and remain creative only with a conscious development of form and aesthetics. You cannot design with techniques alone. This continues a rich seam in *AD*'s history, as reflected by the presence of Peter Cook, who has contributed to these pages since he co-founded Archigram in the mid-1960s and influenced many of its contributors as a designer and an educator. Often fascinated by technology and gadgetry, he has remained foremost a creative, concerned with design rather than science or software.

In true *AD* style, this title is also challenging. Whether you agree or not it begs a response. Its emphasis on the artistic and the expressive possibilities of architecture – perhaps most pronounced in Yael Reisner's article – will certainly gain as much empathy as it does opposition. In its new format, *AD* will remain as committed, if not more so, to asking questions and to delivering crosscurrents alongside currents. The forthcoming fourth issue of this year (July/August 2010), *The New Structuralism: Design, Engineering and Architectural Technologies*, guest-edited by Rivka and Robert Oxman, could be regarded as the foil to this issue, arguing for the convergence of structural engineering and design and the hegemony of a new structuring logic in design, overriding the purely creative. **AD**

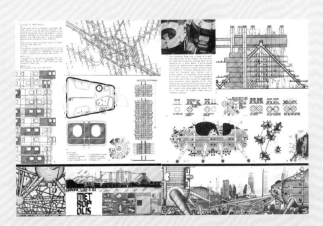

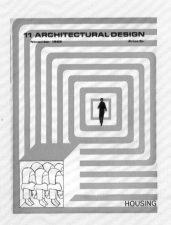

Double-page spread from 'Archigram Group, London: A chronological survey', *Architectural Design*, November 1965, pp 559–73. Peter Cook made his debut in AD in 1965, as a co-founder of Archigram, in a 15-page feature dedicated to the group's work.

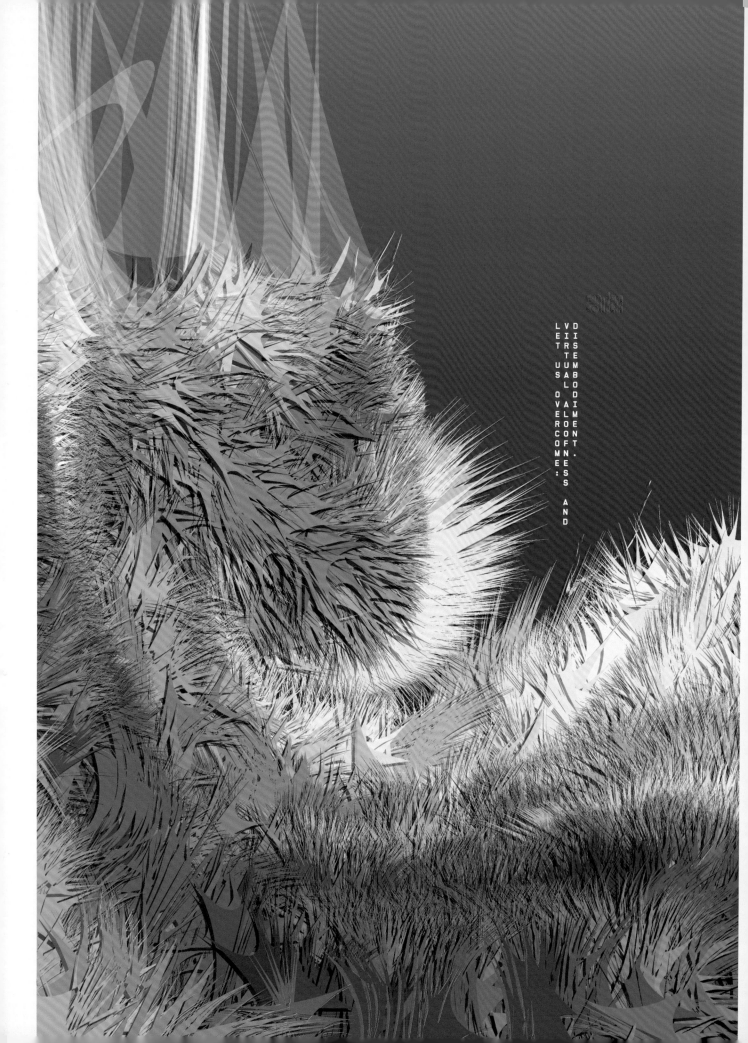

LET US OVERCOME: VIRTUAL DISEMBODIMENT AND DATALOGICAL SOFTNESS AND.

Dr Marjan Colletti is co-founder of the studio marcosandmarjan in London, and currently a lecturer in architecture at the Bartlett School of Architecture, University College London (Unit Master, Unit 20), and the University of Westminster (Unit Master, DS10) with Marcos Cruz. He has been a guest professor at UCLA and Innsbruck University, Austria and design instructor at various institutions in Europe and Asia. His projects and texts attempt to bridge the gap between architectural theory and the built environment by expanding the vocabulary of digital architecture. On various platforms – research, education and practice – he endeavours to establish a debate in which experimentation, technology and innovation do not exclude personal emotions, local traditions and cultural identity. His work has been widely published and shown in more than 50 exhibitions in Europe, Brazil and Asia.

marcosandmarjan's portfolio includes the competition-winning entry for a 180,000-square-metre (1.9 million-square-foot) entertainment complex in front of the gates of the Summer Palace in Beijing, the built pavilions and general layout for the 2005 Lisbon Book Fair, as well as the ongoing NURBSTERS series and the runner-up project for an estate Sales Centre and model homes display in Cairo. Marjan's PhD on 'Digital Poetics' (Bartlett, UCL), the co-authored book *marcosandmarjan: Interfaces/Intrafaces* (SpringerWienNewYork, 2005) and the print collection *2&1/2D Twoandahalf Dimensionality* (Bucher Hohenems, 2006) favour a poetic digital avant-garde developed through 2-D, 3-D software and computer numerically controlled (CNC), rapid protoyping (RP), and computer-aided design and computer-aided manufacturing (CAD/CAM) technologies. Parallel strands of research are developing novel morphologies (Convoluted Tectonics), new urban strategies (InterPolis), higher education syllaba in digital design, computation and technology (AC_DC Architectural Curriculum for Design Computing), as well as sustainable manufacturing strategies (InterTech). ∆

Marjan Colletti, 2&1/2D Fluffy Blue One: 'Let us overcome virtual aloofness and disembodiment', 2006
The infinite digital space formed in computer-aided design can most precisely be described by splinear, 2&½D drawings that convey more intricate spatial attributes than simple 2-D line drawings, yet less than 3-D renderings. Such drawings remain geometrically infinitely flat, yet they appear spatial in the manifestation of surfaces, volumes and shadows.

Marjan Colletti, 3&1/2D Shiny One, 2009
Unforeseen behaviours of circles-lofts are developed as part of an 'anexact' design process that employs otherwise exact and precise CAD commands. The results are abstract and symbolic; digital constructs – fictional metareproductions – of something between nature and technology, between the known and the unknown, the imaginary and the real. The digital architect is understood as being capable of acting and (meta)producing artistically since engagement with the model demands aesthetic consideration of its properties.

Marjan Colletti, Bartsters installation, Prague-Bratislava-Kosice, 2004–05
marcosandmarjan's NURBSTERS are a series of models and 1:1 prototypes, conceived for exhibitions and installations. The design and manufacturing processes are completely computerised. The Bartsters (Bartlett Nurbsters), designed as exhibition islands especially for the Bartlett/ British Council exhibitions in Prague, Bratislava and Kosice in 2004 and 2005, challenge the dichotomy of style/structure. Building up a complex object, and fitting programmatic, structural, ergonomic requisites expressed through curvilinear and arabesque geometries, the assemblage technique reinterprets the traditional Chinese wooden cut-joint fitting ideal for quick assembly and disassembly.

EXUBERANCE AND DIGITAL VIRTUOSITY

In the history of civilisation there have been regular waves of various manifestations of exuberance – in architecture, in the arts, in politics, in religion, in philosophy, in economics and so on – preceded and followed by more austere, spartan, strict periods. In architecture alone there have been too many styles, movements and individual architects that have pursued an exuberant, expressive, expansive vocabulary to possibly give an introductory historic account of exuberance. Thus it seems more appropriate to disclose the brief history of *Exuberance*, this very magazine. As it takes a considerable, but not excessive, amount of time to compile an issue of *AD*, at face value the guest-editor's bias behind title and content should not happen to change within the time frame between first draft proposal and publishing. Also, it is unlikely that the whole context per se would change. Yet this it what happened during the development of this issue. Twice. Perhaps the effect of those ripples that are formed in proximity of larger waves.

Exuberance: Protest-Manifesto-Celebration
At its conception, *Exuberance* was a protest. It was concocted to present a digital world of architecture that antagonised the engineered understanding of digital performance. The term was chosen for its politically incorrect bias – not optimised, not modulated, not algorithmic – and as a selection tool for filtering out most of the 'techy' and 'geeky' talk. Against such trends, I envisioned an issue that heralded a new era of exuberance in digital design. Having overcome the alienation and otherness of the cyber, having mastered the virtual qualities and protocols of the parametric, having achieved the intricacy and elegance of the digital, and having fully embraced the potential of 3-D computer software and CAD/CAM manufacturing technologies, it was now time for architects, not engineers and programmers, to show off.

But then something seemed to be changing. Those clear and clever ideas that initially a few intelligent and very influential people were articulating became more repetitive and were copied intensively – daily routine in many architecture schools, in offices, in exhibitions. Just too mainstream to be avant-garde? The empiricist barricade got more crowded and hence got weakened. A different intelligentsia began articulating other digital things beyond engineered skins, and the few digital phenomenologists (myself included) rejoiced. The system seemed to open up, to become more inclusive; more interpolated, inquisitive, impatient; more Baroque, even Rococo (Rococo being the feminine moment of the Baroque).

And more excessive, extravagant, exuberant. Thus *Exuberance* turned into a manifesto. Of the pervasiveness of phenomenological aspects of digitality, of the varied approaches towards digital design, of the non-engineered intelligence of digital space, of the profuseness of digi-bio-techno ornamentation, of the abundance of CGI in Hollywood, of the excessiveness of computer games, of the lavishness of Middle Eastern and Asian super-urbanism. But also of fluidity and elegance, of a rather sinister neo-*Jugendstil* revival, even of a neo-Rococo 'prettynisation' of the digital: the coloration had shifted towards darker greys and greens, as well as brighter pinks and blues. Morphological complexity was often applied – consciously – as decoration, and digital design intruded into bourgeois homes in the shape of teapots, lamps and coffee mugs.

A few months later, three main events in economics, politics and environmental sciences raised more serious new questions on what *Exuberance* might be. The global banking breakdown and financial crisis marked the end of the latest 'irrational exuberance' period of the stock market.[1] The election of Barack Obama as President of the United States personified the need for change of American and international policies. Simultaneously, the overdue political and economic acknowledgment of the acute seriousness of global climatic changes simply gave us no choice but to think consciously: lower energy consumption, reconsider aesthetics and push sustainability. Suddenly, the Baroque macho excessive and the Rococo feminine pretty tail of digital architecture seemed endangered by these three concurrent events. Were we witnessing the initial sparks of a neo-Enlightened spirit that would mark the end of digital prodigality, luxury and exuberance, albeit in its early stages?

In general terms, a few parallels with the beginning of the 18th century could be drawn.

First, just over two hundred years ago Enlightened politics triggered the French Revolution and saw the monarchy as wasting resources. In recent times, was not former president George W Bush impersonating a Baroque monarch, the figure of the hero and the saint, fusing church and state, religious fanaticism and undisciplined passions (war) together to keep hierarchical status? And was not the feminine Rococo moment in recent politics Condoleezza Rice serving as Secretary of State and Hillary Clinton's campaign in the Democratic primary in the 2008 presidential race?

Marjan Colletti, 2&1/2D
The Intricate One, 2006
Gradients and shadows,
line widths, strokes and
their colours – deep
appearances.

Second, Enlightened economics separated art from luxury, bourgeois saving from spending as status symbol, taste from fashion. The economists rejected the established hierarchies of the sword over the law over finance.[2] In present times, are not many governments spending enormous sums of money on wars? Is not the bailing-out process of the banking system being claimed as the end of excess, of luxury and (super)capitalism; as a trend towards socialism, morality and modernisation?

Finally, Enlightened agronomics saw agriculture as the most virtuous and useful art, the way forward back to nature and romantic sensibility, as well as to productivity and investment. Nowadays, is not the decision of governments to cut down carbon emissions and greenhouse gases, and in future the intense focus on the bio – biotechnology, bioengineering – inevitable?

Consequently, the question raised spontaneously: did such a global downturn imply the end of exuberance? On the contrary. Digital exuberance is not to be misunderstood as luxury, superfluity or prodigality; neither is it the same as extravagant, weird, eccentric. Exuberant here equals energy, enthusiasm, excitement and encouragement. Optimism. Thus, with the context having somersaulted twice, *Exuberance* became what it is now hopefully stronger, and certainly timely. Not a protest, not a manifesto, but a celebration. Of the prodigy, generosity and ingenuity of digitality and of architecture in general, and of the talent, the spirit and the virtuosity of some of its protagonists.

Digital Virtuosity

The celebration of exuberance defines an architecture that begins where common sense ends. With the ambition to establish conditions beyond the usual, the known, the rational, the obvious and the simple. In the current global situation, the biggest danger lies in giving up creativity for inventiveness. It could be argued that architecture is not good at inventing things; engineering, philosophy and politics of course do it better. But it is unbeaten in its ability to create, rediscover and reinvent itself, the environment and the human spirit. In fact, the issue debates a plethora of intelligent ways in which experimental architecture manages to cope with the contemporary turmoil in global politics, economics and ecology. Here occurs the wonder: 'stuff' we are mostly familiar with is stretched to its absolute extent. Common sense becomes the experiment; beauty becomes the sublime, the

grotesque, the blissful; the digital becomes the experiential; the anecdotal, the non-techy and non-geeky. Bring forth the new virtuosos (although curiously some of them happen to be the old masters, and some others still students).

In 'Interiorities' (pp 24–31), Ali Rahim confesses the purpose to generate architecture as rich in its 'level of designed luxury', 'coherence and precision of formal organisation' as the best-known precedents; yes even 'the most filigree Gothic spaces or the most exuberant Baroque or Rococo interiors'. In 'Surrealistic Exuberance – Dark Matters' (pp 64–69), Neil Spiller explores the exuberant dark eroticism and its poetic potential of Baroque and religious imagery, and exploits them in the narratives and design of his Communicating Vessels project.

In 'Cultivating Smartcities' (pp 96–103), CJ Lim calls out for 'a new formal, textural and experiential exuberance' of urbanity with nature – a sensibly exuberant approach to deal with the exorbitant demand for food, and space, in the Far East. While in 'Relying on Interdependencies' (pp 88–95), Kjetil Trædal Thorsen and Robert Greenwood mandate architects to 'act within the spirit of cooperation and dialogue, alongside contemporary values without compromising long-term qualities or architectural integrity'. The featured King Abdulaziz Center for Culture and Knowledge is a showcase project for how environmentally complex scenarios like the Middle Eastern desert can be engaged with by imaginative solutions far beyond common sense.

In 'Baroque Exuberance: Frivolity or Disquiet?' (pp 44–49), Robert Harbison introduces us to some of the many 'facile games', or 'profound exposures', that the Baroque spirit staged. The Baroque wish to defy gravity echoes also in Wolf D Prix's article 'Let's Rock over Barock' (pp 50–57), which highlights a cultural phenomenon of Austrian 'space inventors': the 'desire to celebrate space'.

In 'Exuberance, I Don't Know; Excess, I Like' (pp 70–77), Hernan Diaz Alonso links exuberance to emergent qualities and to the notion of affect, yet at the same time rejects it for excessiveness and arousement; aspects of greater intensities in his work. Also more towards the extreme than the exuberant tends Tom Wiscombe's 'Extreme Integration' (pp 78–89), its performance depending on 'messiness, excess and jungle thinking'.

In 'Diving into the Depth-Scape: Exuberance and Personalities' (pp 32–39), Yael Reisner states that it is 'personality, character and poetics' that 'take part in exuberant expression'. The article is a clear invocation for emotion

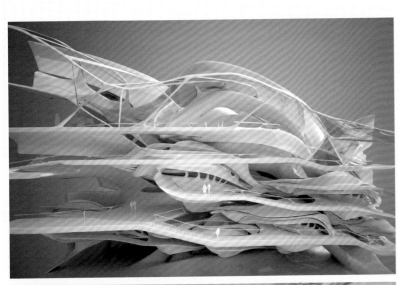

and intuition, evocatively illustrated by her *Depth-Scape Interactive Time-cycled Light & Acoustic installation* project. Personality does certainly come across in fashion design, where couturiers are more often than not eccentrics. In 'Exuberant Couture' (pp 40–45), Judith Clarke, reveals that in fashion 'exuberance, in order to stay exuberant, is always seeking new forms', as it is 'by definition performative'.

For decades Peter Cook has lectured on cheerfulness in architecture, and his *oeuvre* will leave an astonishing legacy of exuberant, flamboyant, clever projects. Out of his 'creative tank', *New Delfina*, purposely designed for this issue, did 'burst forth' (see pp 58–59). My own articles feature mostly student work produced in Unit 20 at the Bartlett School of Architecture at University College London, DS10 at the University of Westminster,[3] and Innsbruck University; hopefully similarly exuberant, flamboyant and clever.

In conclusion, I can reveal that it is no coincidence that such a motley crew has one common characteristic (that all contributors are educators and hence good communicators), that *Exuberance* questions small and large scale (complexity on many layers), that the issue includes fashion, building and urban design (the pervasiveness of the digital), that some opinions differ (it is neither a protest nor a manifesto), that some aesthetics are sinister-dark and some other more romantic-flowery (the non-techy, non-geeky talk), that some texts are more theoretical and others more practical (crossing the boundaries between academia and practice), that it is indebted to Baroque theatricality – similarly playful, ebullient and slightly arrogant. But then again, as it emerges from new media and novel technologies, its palimpsest (to use 20th-century television terms) is more of a variety show than a theatre performance or a documentary. In truth, more of a reality TV show, really: only apparently unscripted, in truth heavily edited and post-produced. ∆

Notes
1. 'Irrational exuberance' was the term Alan Greenspan, Chairman of the US Federal Reserve Board, first used on 5 December 1996 to describe the speculative mania of the 1990s stock market.
2. For further reading see Rémy G Saisselin, *The Enlightenment Against the Baroque: Economics and Aesthetics in the Eighteenth Century*, A Quantum Book, University of California Press (Berkeley, CA and Oxford), 1992, pp 72–3.
3. Unit 20 at the Bartlett School of Architecture and DS10 at the University of Westminster in London are both run by Marjan Colletti and Marcos Cruz. Other work by these studios has been published previously in *AD Protoarchitecture* and *AD Neoplasmatic Design*.

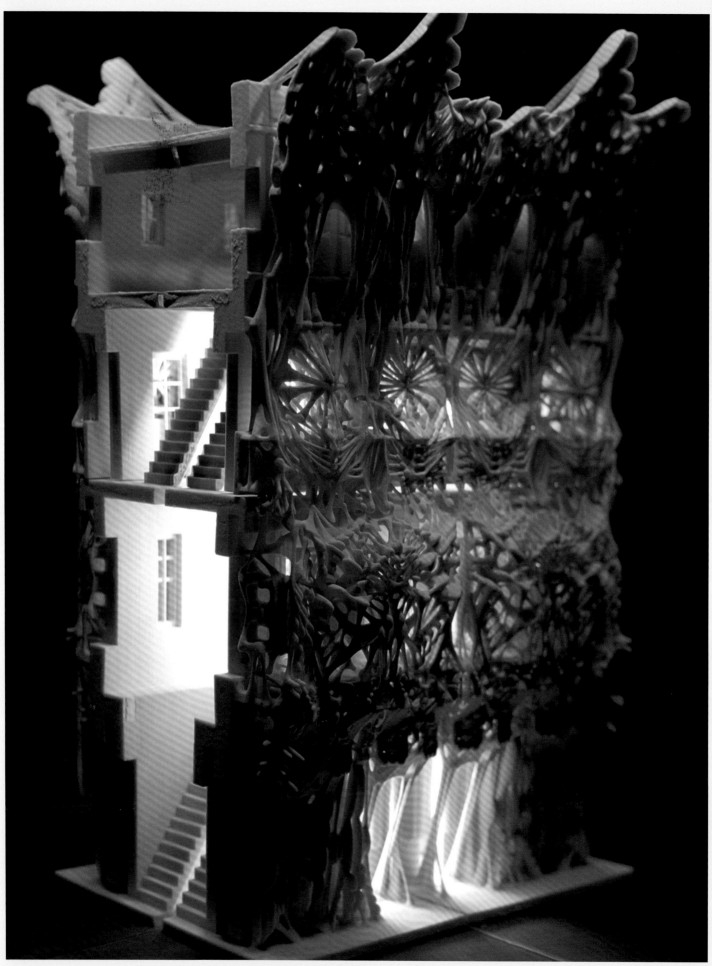

Yousef Al-Mehdari (Unit 20, Bartlett School of Architecture, UCL), The New Polyhydric Body, 2008–09
below: The New Polyhydric Body study attempts to reinterpret the complexity of overlapping anatomies through repeated and non-scripted digital computations (such as extrusions, rotations and progressive scaling) in order to generate new types of architectural form. 'Polyhydra' is a generative term deriving from *poly* (literally, multi), and *Hydra* (the many-headed serpent).

Tobias Klein (Unit 20, Bartlett School of Architecture, UCL), Synthetic Syncretism/Our Lady of Regla Chapel, Havana, 2005–06
opposite: The narrative background is based upon the hybrid Cuban Santeria religion – a mixture of Catholicism and saints, and African Yoruba tribe beliefs and animal sacrifices. Due to lack of burial space in Havana, a ceremonial processional funerary route through the city is proposed. Slotted inside an existing cross-shaped courtyard, the inverted chapel acts as an architectural highlight. Its formal and structural expression is provided by a series of designed Santerian relics held inside the sacristy – skeletal and visceral utensils, 3-D modelled and 3-D printed in order to perfectly fit 3-D-scanned animal bones.

Graham Thompson (Unit 20, Bartlett School of Architecture, UCL), Synthetic Sustainability – Bio-Farm, Turin, Italy, 2008–09
right and bottom: The biotech centre proposal includes a biofuel production facility to explore new ways of breeding strains of algae to produce a sustainable biofuel that can be employed in the depleting fossil-fuel market. Left: Detail of nutrient intent soft system. Pliant adaptive parts are responsive and evolve – specific mechanisms help maintain the health of the living capillaries and their internal growth status. Right: Detail of bio-robotic machine consisting of multifunctional and rotational amateurs. These artificially intelligent machines are programmed to maintain and increase lush synthetic growth within an architectural bioscaffold.

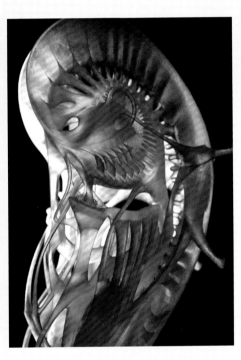

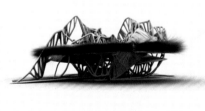

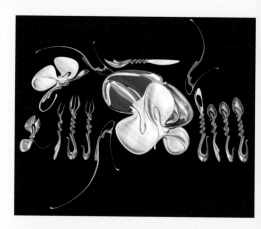

Eoin O'Dwyer (DS10, University of Westminster), New Egyptian National Assembly, Cairo, 2008–09
left: Aerial view of central courtyard. The project explores the relocation of the Egyptian National Assembly from its existing site. The introverted aspect of light filtering into the living areas of a traditional Arabic house through the central courtyard provides the contextual focus. Light is explored using a single light-wave source model to generate contour lines radiating out in different directions from one central source. This is then multiplied, creating opposing forces and developing into a series of physical models, providing the basis for a structural, light diffusing roof system for the main council building.

Xefirotarch, Tableware product design, 2009
left: Tableware by Hernan Diaz Alonso. Far from being virtual, digital design embraces all scales, from the urban to product design or even jewellery. File-to-factory design protocols, combined with exuberant stylistic expressions, also seem to attract major international product companies.

marcosandmarjan, Self-Sufficient City: Khataba (Al Jadida) Agropolis, Egypt, 2009
The rapid increase in the population of the Nile Delta, especially around Cairo and Alexandria, is forcing hundreds of thousands of people into peripheric and unsustainable satellite developments. This is happening either in the desert in enclosed condominiums for the rich, or in the Delta in shanty-town-like settlements for the poor. The proposed new self-sufficient towns along the Delta are intended to redirect the uncontrolled urban sprawl into new agro-urban settlements that grow in accordance with local farming activity. The Agropolis is self-sufficient in terms of the involvement of the local population, new transport infrastructures, programme mix and, above all, a sustainable balance in food and energy production and consumption.

Steven Ma (Graduated Thesis programme: advisor Hernan Diaz Alonso, Southern California Institute of Architecture/sci-arc), Xuberant, 2008
below: he project investigates how calligraphical aesthetics and the formal language of exuberance can create effects through the production of liminality. The form is created by constantly evolving the relationship between systems that are held in maximal tension in relation to one another, suspended in a permanent state of incomplete transition. New speciation thus evolves. It is this 'in-between state' of mutation that allows multiple systems to generate infinite growth. Stylistic individuation becomes the contemporary meaning of style.

DIGITALIA – THE OTHER DIGITAL PRACTICE

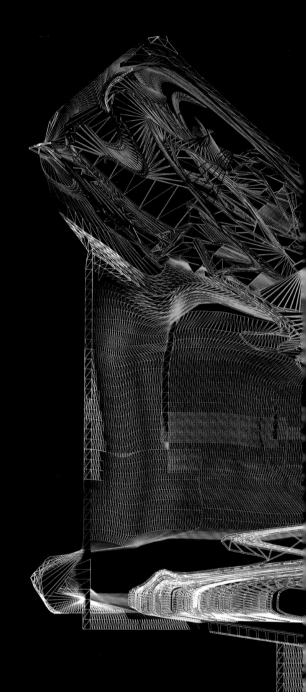

Hannes Mayer (Unit 20, Bartlett School of Architecture, UCL), Lichonic Architecture, 2007–08
The design is driven by image-based vector fields that break with the convention of the line as a border. Binary space is replaced by gradients of enclosure. Reference image layers are stacked on top of each other to create a three-dimensional colour cloud. Architecture emerges in these fields as a result of discreetly interpolated forces. Despite the exuberance of the final product, the whole design is driven by quick and simple sketches and images.

Marjan Colletti, the guest-editor of this issue, defines a clear political agenda for DigitAlia as an alternative mode of digital practice. He outlines how it potentially absorbs the latest digital techniques while embracing the poetic and knowledge of cultural traditions and pushing the very boundaries of creativity. The scope of Colletti's ideas is illustrated by images from his own practice with Marcos Cruz, marcosandmarjan architects, and those of his students at the Bartlett School of Architecture (UCL), the University of Westminster in London and Innsbruck University in Austria.

The pursuit of computerised complexity per se is, at present, most often a rather shallow endeavour. Elaborated topological 3-D crochets appear as frequently on the Internet as 3-D rendered chimeras and monsters. Indeed, the first are good enough for copy-and-paste blogs, the latter for 3-D software gallery pages. But surely, this issue's quest for (digital) exuberance does not pertain to either group of these skilled modellers.

Neither does exuberance concern the rationalist and epistemological lobby: its barricades crowded and piled high; its manifestos engineer-functionalist, mathematic-descriptive and neo-*Sachlich*. Against this trend, I bring forth the possibility of an empiricist phenomenological counterpart: DigitAlia – the other digital practice. It adheres to the principles of openness and synthesis, and favours a digital avant-garde developed through 3-D software and computer numerically controlled (CNC), rapid prototyping (RP), computer-aided design and computer-aided manufacturing (CAD/CAM) technologies. DigitAlia has no manifesto, as it does not believe in dogmas, doctrines and isms, yet it has a clear political agenda, which is outlined below:

1. Digital Politics
The politics of DigitAlia are inclusive and involve everything that is to do with digitality: practice, profession, methods, manoeuvres, principles, opinions, strategies, intrigue, and control over structure, organisation and administration.

2. Digital Poetics
DigitAlia provides an alternative to the understanding and the production of CAD beyond protocols, mathematics and geometry, and towards digital poetics: performance, (re)production, (re)presentation, projection, mimesis, automatism, reflection and bliss, intuition, creativity and intimacy.

3. Convolution
DigitAlia equals convolution (blur, overlap and interference): it expands architecture by blurring and pushing the boundaries of the discipline, by layering contexts, ideas and technologies, and by multitasking and by interfering with linear design processes.

4. CAADemiurgy
DigitAlia reproposes the digital architect as demiurge: the creator and craftsman, whose skills manage to call into being possible spaces, places, images, things, words and worlds that are not, with a plethora of means of representation and of Technik not available to the analogue practice.[1]

5. CyberBaroque
DigitAlia avoids the dichotomy of rational and empirical thinking, and enables the morphing of classical-digital architectural semantics into playful theatrical tectonics and typologies. In fact, the most contemporary manifestation of digital architecture achieves the synthesis of poetic expression and intuitive knowledge, of culture and tradition as well as industry and progress.

6. Phenomenology
DigitAlia does not dismiss a phenomenological inspection into CAD's personal, subjective, intellectual and cognitive processes. On the contrary, the phenomenological goal for DigitAlia is twofold: the phenomenology of the poetic imagination (of the designer and the user), and of the poetic image (of the architectural input and output).[2] Such poetic digital image achieves the overlap of intuition/input and expression/output.[3]

7. Cognitive Parameters
DigitAlia aims at merging geometric parameters and cognitive properties, as well as geometric properties and cognitive parameters. Geometric properties are to do with materiality, form, organisation – the setup of *Gestalt*; cognitive parameters are to do with senses, perception, behaviour – the setup of consumption (or even empathy). The latter include anamorphic projections, perspectival illusion, environmental criteria and other perception-based parameters.

8. Approximatively Rigorous
When architecture is understood as an approximately exact dynamic morphological entity – as variations in decisions and process do inevitably produce different outputs – rigour is the approximatively exact coming to terms with an anexact yet definitely maybe rigorous process: the coming to terms with ambiguity towards control by extrapolating individual observations towards a common strategic agenda and social proposal.

9. Exuberance
Criticising objectivity as invariance, evolution as method, users as observers, it could be argued that it is the challenge of this generation

of creative thinkers (whatever the discipline) to fully engage
with the actuality – rather than the virtuality – of CAD. This
means that after the initial period of definition and discovery
of disembodied virtual realities, datascapes and cyber-
realities, the endeavour now is to establish a debate in which
experimentation, technology and progress do not exclude the
actuality of emotions, traditions and identity – and the pursuit
of exuberance.

10. InterPolis – Interpolated Urbanism

Pursuing an interpolating research strategy that is synthetic –
as it introduces something new between an array of existing
elements – results in the emergence of InterPolis. Digital
urbanism usually extrapolates geometric singularities into
multiplicity and modulation of complexity/language via
parametric cohesion. Such an approach is global, and pursues
networking, evolution and growth. InterPolis approaches
urbanism by interpolating multiplicity and modulation of
complexity/language into singularity via convoluted cohesion.
Such an approach is also global, as it pursues identity,
involution (involvement) and synthesis. 𝄐

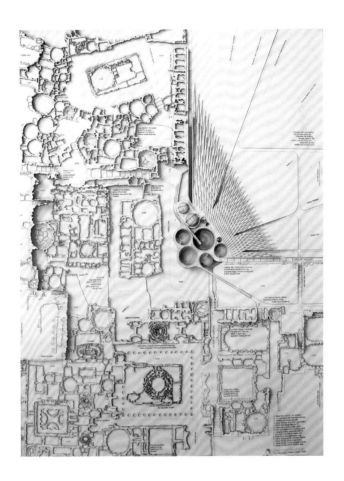

Notes
1. The CAADemiurge can overcome the schisms in the 15th and 16th
centuries between intellectual and manual labour (and architecture), and
in the 19th century between automatic mechanisation and poetic creation.
The operational field of the demiurge is the 'choros, the precosmic space,
the place and the "nurse" of all being'. See Joseph Rykwert, *The Dancing
Column: On Order in Architecture*, MIT Press (Cambridge, MA and London),
1996, p 386.
2. In contrast to Jesse Reiser and Nanako Umemoto, phenomenology is here
not dismissed as 'the desire to have everything grounded within the body
and within experience', and I do not agree that 'phenomenological practice
could never propose a new architecture'. Reiser and Umemoto claim that
phenomenology is not good enough as a 'generative model', and that if it
were, then architecture would lapse 'into some form of modernism for the
purpose of organizing space' and some sort of classical model of humanism.
See Jesse Reiser and Nanako Umemoto, *Atlas of Novel Tectonics/Reiser +
Umemoto*, Princeton Architectural Press (New York), 2006 pp 230, 84.
3. Very much in line with Gaston Bachelard and his poetic reverie,
it demands active participation and intuitive response during design
production. See Gaston Bachelard, *The Poetics of Reverie: Childhood,
Language, and the Cosmos*, trans Daniel Russell, Beacon Press (Boston,
MA), 1971, pp 183–210. And it seems to look 'for salient "poetic"
(*cultural*) and not merely scientific-rational (technical) proponents of the
digital revolution'. See Mark Goulthorpe, 'Notes on digital nesting: A poetics
of evolutionary form', in Leon van Schaik, *AD Poetics in Architecture*, Vol
72, No 2, March 2002, p 19.

Sam White (Unit 20, Bartlett School
of Architecture, UCL), Chapel to the
Corpus, Wells, Somerset, 2004–05
below: This proposal for an extension
to Wells Cathedral creates a scene for
the cult of the body. People come to it
as a place of worship, while suspended
scaffolds of human form and mechanical
support systems are used for the
production of surgical flesh supplies.

Johan Voordouw (Unit 20,
Bartlett School of Architecture, UCL),
Aedicules, Tivoli, Italy, 2007–09
opposite top: A woven sequence of
aedicules creates a memory archive,
continuously and simultaneously oscillating
between hidden and revealed chambers
and labyrinths. The public archive
bridges an existing stair in the town, the
private archive is carved into the soft
travertine hillside and requires more active
participation, and in the archive's library,
memories get organised, catalogued and
stored. A rapid-prototyped book narrates
the experiential aspects of the project and
reveals the atmospherics, the wonderment
or burden that secrets may contain.

Peter Griebel (Studio Colletti, Innsbruck
University, Austria), Santa Mira La Guapa,
San Carlo alle Quattro Fontane, Rome, 2007
below: The project focuses on reinventing the
character of Baroque churches, in particular
Borromini's San Carlo alle Quattro Fontane.
Context, scale and programme remain close
to the original. The exuberant interior is bent
and compressed, and extends towards the
'lobotomised' exterior, which is shaped by
forces different to those inside.

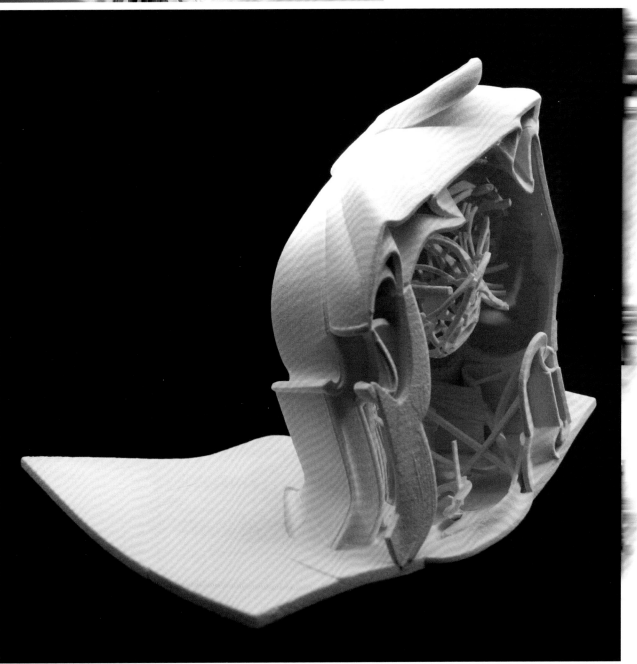

Kasper Ax (Unit 20, Bartlett School of Architecture, UCL), Tooling – Ecumenical Council, Turin, Italy, 2008–09
below left and right: Constructed viewpoints are created to infuse the spatial configurations with distorted and exaggerated perspectives as well as figurative means. In the case of the interior of the Ecumenical Council of Turin, this theory is employed in viewpoints where certain panels in the ceiling are extracted and treated with a distinct materiality that enables the beholder to interpolate figures, such as the cross, in the mind.

Kapil Amarnani Chawla (DS10, University of Westminster), New Cairo Sustainable Development, 2007–08
right: The scheme consists of an urbanisation in between a number of centre-pivotal irrigation farms. The circular farms use an advanced irrigation method that creates a final product that is on average 28 per cent more efficient than traditional methods can achieve. Based on studies of the typologies of the farms – their internal paths, watering systems and even their connections to aquifers – the scheme merges and blends these pockets of food with the needs of the city.

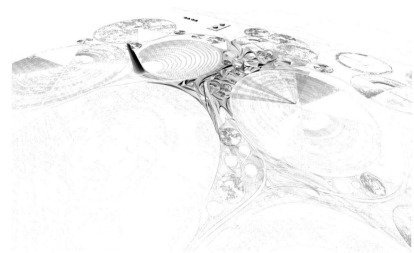

Oliver von Malm (Studio Colletti, Innsbruck University, Austria), New Johann Nepomuk Chapel, Asamkirche, Munich, 2007
below left: A new chapel is inserted into the exuberant yet tiny interiors of the Asam church. The facade in-folds into the church, absorbs the character of the twisted columns above the altar, and intersects itself. Heavy, curved Baroque surfaces emerge from the geometric topological and functional parameters of the built context. They accelerate the reflections of the sunlight falling into the chapel and give the impression of infinity by forcing the observer to lose himself within the chapel's infinite folds.

Vicky Patsalis (Unit 20, Bartlett School of Architecture, UCL), Screaming Architecture, 2007–08
below right: This proposal draws on the representative emotions of a human for its physiognomic reading, necessitating a formal understanding of the human body as well as requiring empathy from its viewer; empathy with regards to the scream, which simultaneously indulges and divulges each circumstantial viewing of the arcade. Attempting to restore and rethink the figural relationship with architecture, the design investigation learns from the flaws of its classical predecessors to reflect the current age of aesthetics in its terrifying sublime.

INTERIO

Ali Rahim

RITIES

Ali Rahim emphasises the importance for design of overlaying a mastery of digital techniques with a nuanced and developed aesthetic sensibility. Here he illustrates his fascination with the formal with his exploration of 'interiorities', or internal logics of tectonic structures, in his design research at the University of Pennsylvania. The strive to create variation and atmosphere in buildings effectively places a stress on different part-to-whole relationships, organisations, material qualities and colours and their various rates of transformation.

Jisuk Lee (Rahim Research Studio, University of Pennsylvania), Migrating Formations: Mixed-Use Complex, Moscow, 2008

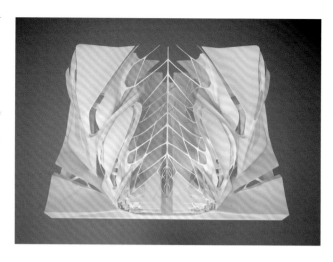

Jisuk Lee (Rahim Research Studio, University of Pennsylvania), Migrating Formations: Mixed-Use Complex, Moscow, 2008
Seduction is about visually enticing someone with a certain kind of aesthetic expression. The aesthetic expression here is defined as 'voluptuousness', conveyed by undulating lines and surfaces; the aesthetic is expressed by transformations between each component and the behaviours of their arrangements. Accumulation of smaller components creates an intricacy that transforms as a larger whole, maintaining a richer effect than as individual units.

Johnny Lin (Rahim Research Studio,
University of Pennsylvania), Interiorities:
Urban Club, TriBeCa, New York City, 2009
The design research tested the limits
of elegance studying quick and slow
transformations in different sequences.
The transformations resulted in the
understanding that if both co-existed in the
overall form of the project, the organisation
would still yield an elegant project. Colour
was also tested, allowing the systemic
relations to highlight specific geometry
in addition to yielding an overall colour
transformation to enhance the affect of the
project on both the interior and exterior.

Cultural and technological innovations establish new status quos and updated platforms from which to operate and launch further innovations to stay ahead of cultural developments. Design research practices continually reinvent themselves and the techniques they use, and guide these innovations to stay ahead of such developments.

Reinvention can come through techniques that have already been set in motion, such as dynamic systems and other open-source software programs that are mined for all their potential, through the development of new plug-ins that are able to change attributes within dynamic systems, or through changing existing or writing new expressions in the form of scripts in computer language – in effect changing the capacity of the operation of the software to develop new techniques for the design and manufacture of architecture. These techniques are important to design research to inform the form, space and material conditions of architecture. All will continue to be developed and alter the way architectural practices operate in the near and long term. Practices can also develop new techniques by investigating new technologies on the horizon of other fields. The necessary characteristics of the technologies selected are that they contain feedback, are interrelational and have the potential to destabilise their current contexts. Techniques borrowed from other spheres can assist architectural practices to become more synthetic, seamlessly integrating the design, testing and manufacture of material formations.

Beyond Techniques to Elegance

The development of techniques is essential for innovation in design. However, the mastering of techniques, whether in design, production or both, does not necessarily yield great architecture. In the Rahim Research Studio at the University of Pennsylvania, Interiorities: An Urban Club for New York City (spring 2009) was an attempt to move beyond techniques by mastering them to achieve nuances within an exuberant formal development of projects that exude an elegant aesthetic sensibility.[1]

Architects who have been able to add such a layer of aesthetic sophistication to their designs share several characteristics that are key to current digital design discourse. All of their projects operate within emerging paradigms of generative techniques, and move past methods completely dependent on the rigorous application of scientific standards. Each exhibits a systemic logic of thought that eschews mapping

Wei Wang (Rahim Research Studio, University of Pennsylvania), Interiorities: Urban Club, TriBeCa, New York City, 2009
The interior of the club is organised by different extents of orientation/disorientation, by manipulating multiple types of geometry and assemblage, purposefully differentiating lighting and materialisation, and synthesising various accumulation strategies and part-to-whole relationships. The organisation and hierarchy of the interior systems constantly inspire and eventually drive the formation and transformation of the building exterior and its response to the constraints of the site. Colour visually enhances the atmospheric transformation and systematic continuity: blue defines the local transition by highlighting the module's boundary, while yellow is continuously distributed throughout the entire building (exterior and interior), guiding the overall movement, activated in different intensities and assembled specifically according to local conditions to maximise the atmospheric effect.

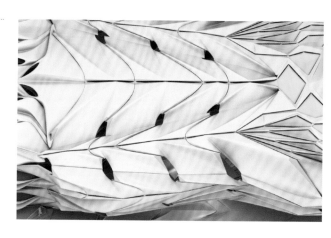

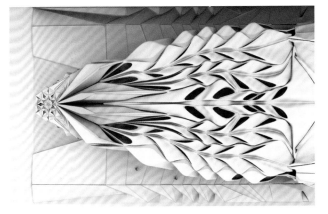

a specific process, or revealing the process of an algorithm being generated, as strategies to generate a project's form. Instead, mastery of the techniques used allows each designer to assume a more sophisticated relationship with the creation of form – using malleable forms differentiated at varied rates that are correlated systemically – a position made possible only through the use of an aesthetic sensibility concomitant with a highly developed design ability.

Affective Formations: Interiorities

Architecture generates cultural change by intensifying and inflecting existing modes of inhabitation, participation and use. To accomplish this, architecture must become more responsive, engaging in a relationship of mutual feedback with its users and contexts. In other words it, it must contain 'affects' – the capacity both to affect and be affected. Affects differ from effects, which, in everyday parlance, imply a one-way direction of causality: a cause always precedes its intended effect. Affects, in contrast, suggest a two-way transfer of information and influence between a formation, or work of architecture, and its users and environment. While all works of architecture arguably have effects, certain projects are more prolific than others. The Rahim Research Studio is interested in designing affective formations – works of architecture that maximise their affects and hence responsiveness to users and contexts.

Interiority suggests the focus on the creation of affective formations that unfold and differentiate within the terms of their own internal and perceptual logics. The creation of affects are most clearly pursued by starting with interiors; that is, without immediately developing the architecture with an environment and exposing it to external influences such as gravity, environment and so on. Perceptual logics assist the way one experiences space and form when moving through and around the interiors. The creation of a series of optical illusions from different angles can be amplified developing a visual understanding of form that has a non-linear relationship to the actual geometry.

The aim is, then, to reach the level of designed luxury found, for instance, in the most excessive Baroque or Rococo interiors. The goal is to go beyond all known historical precedents in terms of qualitative differentiation and the intensity of part-to-part and part- to-whole relationships. Another way to express this is to say that we are aiming to build

up a multi-layered complexity with a high degree of differentiation within each visual system and scale with a high level of correlation between the various levels of perception. Each scale of internal differentiation is associated with corresponding or complementary differentiations within other scales. For example, nested scales of material/textural differentiation in relation to a continuous pattern in colour variation allows for an exuberant affect.

Methodology

Three primary trajectories for exploration were employed in developing the Urban Club for New York City design innovation:

1. Technique Development

Students in the Rahim Research Studio used dynamical/generative techniques to understand and develop systemic logics that derive qualitative rates of change or velocity and quantitative amounts of change, such as direction, as well as accumulations and densities of formations. This interrelational software technology uses vectors of magnitude and direction that effect and accommodate threshold conditions of decay and transformation where the geometry of material relations exceeds the capacity for *Gestalt* definition. Some use these systems, or scripting, to map a scientific approach, or incorporate scientific rigour. The students used these systemic techniques to develop studies of the rate of change and enhance knowledge and understanding of formations. The development of this knowledge requires iteration, and through this iteration each student developed his or her own aesthetic sensibility.

2. Aesthetic Development

Each student developed his or her own sensibility for variation using sub-division modelling techniques that were incorporated in the dynamical system using scripting techniques. The goal was to use extreme variation to produce unprecedented architectural effects that flow from topological surfaces, and part-to-part as well as part-to-whole arrangements in extreme variation to produce distinct formal features for interiorities with the morphological continuity to develop a building. The distinct features – soft to bony, for example – enabled the development of spaces with very disparate and discrete spatial, material and lighting qualities that begin to transform into each other to maintain morphological continuity. The projects able to produce the most radical differences with limits within an aesthetic sensibility were the most successful, the challenge always being to move away from component-based logics (which always produce part-to-part relationships) towards topological continuity that loses each part in the development of an entire project. The aesthetic development is crucial to transferring the emphasis of the design to the affects that it produces.

It is the high degree of variation that contributes to an environment that is able to develop the most qualitative difference in the morphological continuity of the project.

Zongshi Liu (Rahim Research Studio,
University of Pennsylvania), Urban Club,
TriBeCa, New York City, 2009
The topology of the continuous surface
is generated from specific localities and
conditions. Iridescent colours highlight
the geometry of the surface. This changes
depending on light intensity and the
movement of the viewer, thus creating an
affect of sensuality.

3. Project Development and Location

The project was developed simultaneously with the development
of aesthetic and technique. Students channelled and facilitated
the design research towards an urban club located in the New
York neighbourhood of TriBeCa, on Varick Street between N
Moore and Franklin Streets, between existing bars and bar/club
hybrid typologies. The design focuses on a cluster of primary
social rooms: lounge, dining room, library, conference room,
ballroom and den. Intentionally very specific, it synthesises
all of these aspects without losing their intensity to create a
complete architectural experience incorporating form, structure,
material, texture, ornament, colour, transparency/opacity and
light and shadow.

The design research featured here yields interesting knowledge
in terms of how to turn a corner on the interior with material
and the exterior with form, while the variation in colour and
lighting systems, as well as the control of part-to-part and
part-to-whole relationships develop very specific atmospheres in
different locations within each project. The spaces are different
in scale, and the difference is exploited using different material
qualities, whether hard or soft, that are accentuated with colour.
The qualitative difference in each space and project is achieved
through a transformation of spatial scale, material qualities,
part-to-whole relationships, seaming pattern, lighting pattern
and colour accents that at the same time remain morphologically
continuous. It is the high degree of variation that contributes
to an environment that is able to develop the most qualitative
difference in the morphological continuity of the project. ⌂

Note
1. Interiorities: An Urban Club for New York City was taught simultaneously in
Ali Rahim's Research Studio at the University of Pennsylvania in Philadelphia,
and at Studio Hadid (tutors: Ali Rahim and Patrik Schumacher) at the
University of Applied Arts, Vienna.

Exuberance is about more than appearance. **Yael Reisner** argues
that it engenders an emotional response. It provides a whole
'depth-scape' of expression by offering extensive qualities that go
beyond the merely practical or the required. Exuberance proffers
a full emotional range from the horrific to the sublime, which
requires complexity but also the presence of creative personalities
who lend personal interpretation to the design process.

DIVING INTO
THE DEPTH-SCAPE
EXUBERANCE AND
PERSONALITIES

Yael Reisner

Yael Reisner with Lorene Faure, *Depth-Scape Interactive Time-cycled Light & Acoustic installation: Blooming*, 2008
A daytime phase of the interactive time-cycled interior installation when materials, colours and textures are displayed as they come. The combination of soft and hard materials brings in the spatial acoustic quality.

Yael Reisner with Lorene Faure,
*Depth-Scape Interactive Time-cycled
Light & Acoustic installation:
Manifold Silhouettes*, 2008
opposite top left: The silhouetted
phase during the day is explored as
an imagery inspired by Caspar David
Friedrich's painting *The Wanderer
Above the Sea of Fog* (1818). The
different phases are controlled by the
inhabitant's choice of atmosphere.

Yael Reisner with Lorene Faure, *Depth-
Scape Interactive Time-cycled Light &
Acoustic installation: Light*, 2008
opposite top right: In its lit phase,
the depth-scape three-dimensional
installation turns from material to
immaterial.

Yael Reisner with Maro Kallimani,
Andy Shaw and Lorene Faure, *Depth-
Scape Interactive Time-cycled Light &
Acoustic installation: Dusk*, 2007
below: The preferred atmosphere
would be drawn in by the inhabitant.
The charged silhouetted phase
is explored here in its darkest
appearance.

It is fascinating that what unifies contemporary exuberant expression in architecture is its outcome and not the process, technique or technology. It is the 'depth-scape' appearance.

Yael Reisner with Maro Kallimani, Andy Shaw and Atelier One, Family House, Tel Aviv, 2004–08
View from under the pergola above the swimming pool looking east towards the rear facade and garden.

The interior 'light-well-wall', which works as a bouncing artificial sky for the *Depth-Scape Interactive Timed-cycled Light & Acoustic installation*. Both features together enhance the sense of interiority of the space.

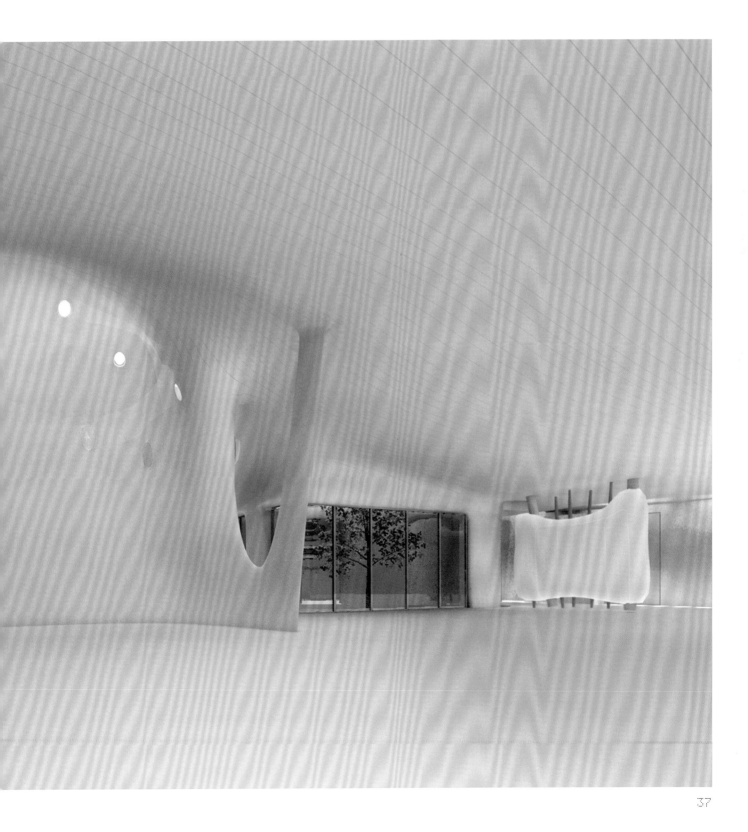

Exuberant architecture is not just about appearance, though some might wish to reduce it to this. It is a means of emotive expression with a wide range of possibilities: from the pleasurable to the horrific, from playfulness and delight via emotional beauty and through to the sublime, where complexity and fulsomeness are conditional characteristics alongside the presence of creative personalities.

One cannot indulge indifferently with exuberant qualities. Emotions and feelings are involved. Exuberance goes beyond practical needs by its very definition. It is about excess and extensive qualities that tend to enthusiastically spill over the balanced requirement.

In the last hundred years exuberant architecture has reappeared cyclically alongside the more sporadic expressions of certain individuals.[1] Abundance was a common theme of the architecture of the German Expressionists[2] in the first two decades of the 20th century. Then, Modernism's early effort towards an aesthetic of universal abstraction in architecture turned into utilitarian design, with personal expression commonly ridiculed as an imposition of individual will on the public realm. It is therefore no wonder that it was 50 years before exuberance reappeared in the Deconstructivist architecture of the 1980s, when feeling and emotions took on a genuine and authentic role in the design process and were evident in the outcome. However, the MOMA 'Deconstructivist Architecture' exhibition, conducted by Mark Wigley's curatorial interpretation in 1988, twisted historical reality by underplaying the emotional facet,[3] a move which appealed to many others involved in the architectural discourse at the time.

During the mid-1990s, the impulse of digital architects was expressed in the fusion of content and structure with form. They were preoccupied with appearance while adopting Modernist non-determinist ethics, this time through the very nature of the digital procedural design process that valued only the objectifying, automated, pseudo-scientific design methods with added threads intrinsic to mathematical computational procedures. Personalities were ridiculed again.[4]

More than a decade later this ethical piety of depersonalisation continues, and is evident in, for example, Neil Leach's recent discussion of performative architecture in which he draws distinctions between the dubious 'form giver' and the positive 'form finder', where the form finder is 'the architect as the controller of generative processes, where the final appearance is a product not of the architect's imagination alone, but of the generative capacities of computer programs.'[5]

Strangely, the use of one's free imagination, let alone personal judgement imbued with creative insight, has been perceived as architecture's arch enemy. Hence Leach brings a clichéd, false and hostile interpretation of Frank Gehry's design process into the discussion. Gehry, he says, is: 'the genius creator who imposes form on the world in a top-down process, [where] the primary role of the structural engineer is to make possible the fabrication of the designs of the master architect, as close as possible to his or her initial poetic expression.'[6] Gehry rejects vehemently the notion of the capricious act. Conversely, he believes that signature and democracy are integrally interlinked, and in

fact, that when an architect suppresses his emotions within the design process this is an act that 'talks down to people' and does not allow a full engagement with architecture.[7]

It is puzzling that these days so many architects still opt to focus and base their creative activity on impersonal knowledge, while in other disciplines and even in current politics a sense of personal judgement is successfully used to communicate one's intentions and win over people's hearts. The President of the United States, Barack Obama, runs his politics within the international arena relying on personal interpretation, as pointed out by BBC 'Newsnight' Diplomatic and Defence Editor Mark Urban after Obama's important Cairo speech in June 2009.[8]

It is our preoccupations – obsessions and passions – that lead us to our most original creative acts. Besides, personal expression is a reflection of one's culture and, eventually, a visual discrimination commenting on a broader, collective cultural spectrum. It is culture and not algorithms and applications of technologies that architectural poetics is evolving from. The aesthetic capacity of architecture is charged by poetic visual qualities that might evoke emotions in the observer.

It is an interesting and testing moment when personality, character and poetics take part in exuberant expression; stemming either from a contemporary digital design process that is no longer objectified, or from a free mix of analogue and digital working methods. It is also satisfying to observe how these days some digital architects go beyond the technical, cerebral and rational approach, and become the new Romantics; a sign of maturity delivered by their gained virtuosity.

Lebbeus Woods, *Stations*, drawing, graphite and coloured pencil on paper, 1989
Throughout the 1980s and 1990s, exuberance and energy were captured through Woods' hand-drawn imagery in his exploration of concepts for a new heroic architecture – grand yet imperfect.

It is fascinating that what unifies contemporary exuberant expression in architecture is its outcome and not the process, technique or technology. It is the 'depth-scape'[9] appearance. It is the spatial-depth quality and effects that are explored, as opposed to the topological surface: continuous and consistent skins. An exuberant 'inside out', three-dimensionally complex with an enhanced depth to be inhabited or involved with at close distance. Since 1998, through teaching and practice, I have been preoccupied with investigating a 3-D interstitial complex condition that was named only in 2004 as 'depth-scape'; the new imagery preceded the name. *The Depth-Scape Interactive Time-cycled Light & Acoustic installation* (2004–08) explored light cycles travelling around and through 3-D manipulated materials and forms that invade space beyond the surface level and deep into the void; where light would cyclically turn material to immaterial. The aspiration here was to go beyond the tendency towards homogeneity of materials, which merely suits 3-D printing machines and often loses the aesthetic opportunities of material diversity with ramifications on the acoustics of the given space.

The buds of this aesthetic are also found in the more recent projects of Lebbeus Woods, Peter Cook, CJ Lim, marcosandmarjan, Neil Spiller, Philip Beesley, Hernan Diaz Alonso and Tom Wiscombe, to mention just a few. However, while the particularity of this aesthetic arguably unites these projects, each architect works from a diverse range of thoughts while using different design tools and media. New spatial language by its very nature is exuberant. The similarity that suddenly becomes apparent is the classic *Zeitgeist* in action, another affirmation that culture wins over technologies. Thus one can add 'depth-scape exuberance' to the historic precedents of the last hundred years. ⚙

Notes
1. Hans Scharoun's Philharmonie, Berlin (1956), Bruce Goff's Shin'en Kan, Bartlesville, Oklahoma (1956), Jørn Utzon's Sydney Opera House (1959), Frank Lloyd Wright's Guggenheim Museum, New York (1959), Archigram's body of work in London in the late 1960s, Hans Hollein's Schullin Jewellery Shop, Vienna (1972), projects by most of the architects known to be Deconstructivists during the 1980s, Enric Miralles' and Benedetta Tagliabue's Scottish Parliament, Edinburgh (2004), and most of the architects I included in my book: Yael Reisner with Fleur Watson, *Architecture and Beauty: Conversations with Architects About A Troubled Relationship*, John Wiley & Sons (Chichester), 2010.
2. For example, Hans Poelzig's Theatre House, Berlin (1919), or Hermann Finsterlin's *Utopian Architecture* drawings (1920).
3. As Wigley concluded: 'The disquieting is not produced by some new spirit of the age; it is not an unsettled world produced by an unsettled architecture. It is not even the personal angst of the architect, it is not a form of expressionism – the architect expresses nothing here.' Philip Johnson and Mark Wigley, *Deconstructivist Architecture*, The Museum of Modern Art (New York), exhibition catalogue, 1988, p 20.
4. Influenced by Bernard Cache who claimed: 'The architect is an intellectual worker whose mode of production is increasingly governed by digital technologies … [which are] hostile … to all approaches that perpetuate the age-old myth of the capricious architect-artist.' *L'architecture d'aujourd'hui*, 349, Nov/Dec 2003, pp 96–7.
5. See Neil Leach, 'Digital Morphogenesis, *AD Theoretical Meltdown*, Vol 79, No 1, Jan/Feb 2009, p 34.
6. Ibid, p 34.
7. Reisner and Watson, op cit.
8. See *www.bbc.co.uk/blogs/.../palestine_and_the_personal.html.*
9. Yael Reisner coined the terms 'depth-scape' and 'spatial-depth' in 2004, some years after being engaged in their visual qualities.

Is the exuberant confined to architecture? **Judith Clark**, curator and lecturer in the history and theory of fashion, looks into the sartorial equivalent of digital exuberance. She describes how exuberance in fashion is largely performance-based expressed on the catwalk, as epitomised by Hussein Chalayan's dramatic staging of his shows.

EXUBERANT COUTURE

Exuberance is the X factor of millinery; whether the swoop of a feather or a flash of red taffeta, exuberance will express and celebrate your Gina Lollobrigida trying to get out and suppress any internal Margaret Rutherford. In my work with John Galliano at Christian Dior exuberance of line is key and we are constantly inspired by Rene Gruau's illustrations of Monsieur Dior's finest silhouettes of the fifties. Here glamour, fashion and sex were blended into pure excitement, fulfilling the dreams of the audience, and it is still a potent cocktail today.
    Stephen Jones, 2009[1]

John Galliano for Christian Dior, Haute-couture collection, Spring/summer 2009
Hat with plumes by Stephen Jones.

Hamish Morrow, Fashion in Zero Gravity, 2004
opposite: 'The reality of gravitational pull affects
every clothing principle relating to cut, construction,
drape and fabric volume and is ultimately one of
its inescapable guiding influences. In a habitat
free from the force of gravity the problems facing
the design of clothes would require a new set
of solutions and in tandem create a new visual
response.' – Hamish Morrow

Hussein Chalayan, Finale Foam Dresses, Inertia
collection, Spring/summer 2009
below: The five dresses that formed Hussein
Chalayan's Inertia collection finale incorporate within
them the dramatic moment of impact of a hypothetical
car crashing at high speed. The impact translated into
form, the wreckage into decoration. The wind machine
catches the model's hair to continue the viewer's
association with high-speed travel.

If exuberance is about self-delight, delirium,
excess as a kind of innocence, how do we
find its sartorial equivalents? The fashion
industry is as much about the presentation
and representation of fashion as it is about
fashion. Digital media are therefore often an
afterthought or a layering of information on
top of a strictly sartorial working out of shape
and form. The mood of a hypothetical wearer
reprojected on to a gown activating it, moving
it gracefully or flamboyantly is the exuberance
cited by Stephen Jones. His creations with
John Galliano at Dior, the most virtuoso of the
haute-couture world are the most traditionally
constructed, by the *petites mains* of the
atelier. They are crafted so as to lose sight of
their generative logic, their complex pattern.
The excitement is invested in the fabric of the
gowns. Their limits are the limits of the fabric
– its folds and its drapery – and the skills of
the craftsman.

Since 2000, fashion Internet sites
such as SHOWstudio, Tank TV, Hint Mag
and Dazed Digital[2] have given fashion an
afterlife and have broadened the scope of
its representation. It exists in more forms.

(Exuberance, in order to stay exuberant, is
always seeking new forms.) It completely
transforms how we might envisage a dress.
There are the endless famous B-rolls showing
us out-takes, redescribing a moment that is
not climactic but creative, and there is the
playing with another, hypothetical existence
of the gown, not to do with its design but its
behaviour: what if it were to move, be lit and
so on, in these ways? What if gravity were
removed? What if a lightshow were projected
on to the model as she walks? And then there
are the more recent questions about what it
might mean if these re-presentations were
reintroduced into the garment itself, so the
garment could *be* the event, could *act out* an
idea. (Exuberance in fashion is always the
acting out of an idea.)

Significant collaborations have emerged,
such as that between Hussein Chalayan and
Rob Edkins at 2D/3D. Chalayan is largely
credited as being fashion's technological
avant-garde using his collection's finale as
the event of the event: the models perform
the clothes and then the clothes themselves
perform. (Exuberance in fashion is by

definition performative.) In his One Hundred
and Eleven collection for spring/summer
2007, dresses acted out a reflection of the
fashion system itself, its mutating hemlines
and silhouettes presented as quickly
morphing dresses, equipped with battery
pack and controlling chips and minute
geared motors. The choreographed dress, the
dress that zips itself up – that most mundane
of actions is rendered alien.

In his more recent Inertia collection
(spring/summer 2009), Chalayan's dresses
dramatised the impact of a car crash,
with sculptural foam forms emerging from
the model's back creating a new kind of
voluptuousness: not Gina Lollobrigida, not
'natural', but digitally constructed. A new
fetishised code or a new sexuality? **Ð**

Notes
1. Stephen Jones, email to the author, London, July
2009.
2. www.showsrudio.com; http//TankTV./; www2.
hintmag.com; http://dazeddigital.com.

UE
RAN CE:
ITY OR
ET?

Robert Harbison

Robert Harbison defines the Baroque in the 17th and early 18th centuries, which is so often characterised in contrast with the Renaissance by its excess and drama. In doing so, he challenges the reader to consider whether this artful style of subversion, tension, movement, gravity-defying feats and freedom was really one of whimsical frivolity or subversive disquiet.

Gianlorenzo Bernini,
Fountain of Four Rivers,
Rome, 1651
A preposterous wildness in an urban context.

Bernardo Vittone, Santa
Chiara, Bra, Piedmont,
Italy, 1741–2
Punctures in the dome
and adjacent domelets.

Giovanni Battista Piranesi,
Engraving of the 'Basilica'
6th-century Greek temple at
Paestum, southern Italy, 1778
An emotive and aestheticised
approach to ancient remains.

Exuberance in Baroque architecture is often expressed as defiance of gravity, in the cloudscapes overhead in Bavarian Rococo churches, in the punctured domes and vaults of Guarino Guarini and his follower Bernardo Vittone, mainly in Piedmont.

Exuberance in the Baroque, the style dominant in Catholic Europe for most of the 17th and early 18th centuries, is a by-product of the desire to overturn Renaissance fixity, solidity and stable harmony. The subversion is perhaps most complete in short-lived forms like fireworks, but more satisfying in more permanent imitations of spontaneous effusion, ranging from asymmetrical decorative effects in flimsy materials to fluid or unstable geometrical forms like ovals or broken pediments, which are preferred to simpler curves or angles.

In the Baroque, before electricity made bright light cheap and commonplace, fireworks must have produced a much stronger impression on the senses than they do now. Then they often formed a crucial part of expansive displays of the ruler's wealth and power in Baroque capitals like Rome, Turin and Vienna. They are the ultimate ephemera, and contributed to the Baroque love of sudden and momentary artistic effects that take spectators by surprise and sweep them away in a rush of excitement.

There are, of course, less fragile and temporary semi-architectural forms of movement and the momentary, like those employing water – fountains and cascades, for instance, which reach new heights and frequency in the Baroque. Though fountains usually repeat themselves, they still give the sensation of being there, then not there, thus instilling the idea of a world founded on change, through which energy visibly pulses.

A fountain like Bernini's *Four Rivers* transports a wild landscape into the centre of a city, a typical Baroque piece of exuberant impossibility. The seeming naturalism of this confection – its carved plant and animal life formerly brightly coloured – paradoxically increases the theatrical artifice of the strange machine.

Another sort of fountain appears to exist in unlikely symbiosis with the facade of a large building, as at the Trevi in Rome (1732–62), where the continuum of windowed walls with gushing torrents and rough-hewn boulders suggests alarming transformations of civilisation into barbarism. Here, architect and sculptors are pushing the boundary between the two and getting an exhilarating charge from the confusion thus created.

Viewing them from the intended subjective perspective, one can even detect exuberance in the sheets of still water in Baroque gardens like those at Versailles or Sceaux, because outlines of pools are seldom simple geometrical forms but incorporate curves and indentations, imparting a sense of constant change to a visitor circling them. Across these flat surfaces rush or ripple the changing spectacle of distorted reflections of buildings, trees and clouds. Clouds themselves have recently been the subject of surprising studies, interpreted as existing in exuberant freedom from necessities like gravity.

Exuberance in Baroque architecture is often expressed as defiance of gravity, in the cloudscapes overhead in Bavarian Rococo churches, in the punctured domes and vaults of Guarino Guarini and his follower Bernardo Vittone, mainly in Piedmont. Punctures generally occur in just those features of the building one counts on for structural soundness, so they feel pleasantly risky. Through their means one is granted a view of spaces beyond the present enclosure. This unexpected freedom recalls kinds of movement which become trademarks of the later medium of film. In fact, film teems with Baroque possibility in the hands of a director like Max Ophuls – most exuberantly in *Le plaisir* (1952), and *Madame de…* and *Letter from an Unknown Woman* (both 1953) – whose camera glides through a connected series of spaces ignoring obstructions like columns and railings, placed in his way just to show how free we are to override any such impediment to our comprehension of the fluid spatial medium the characters inhabit.

In some literal-minded sense, the punctures in Vittone's domes are flaws, but in later Rococo pulpits or little groups of porcelain figures they increase an exuberant variety of form that persuades us that a rational approach is too narrow to keep up with the richness of reality.

One of the strangest ramifications of the Baroque motif of the rent or puncture is the taste for ruins, which began as an intellectual pursuit in the Renaissance and became thoroughly aestheticised in the centuries that followed, until Piranesi could almost make a career of the depiction of incompleteness in the most ragged form imaginable. It is a striking paradox that the 18th-century ruin-taste,

**Francesco Borromini,
Sant' Ivo, Rome,
1642–60**
Interior of the dome
showing its double
geometry that subverts
the single harmony
of its Renaissance
predecessor.

**Santa Prisca, Taxco,
Mexico, 1750s**
Detail of the altarpiece,
where classical orders
are swamped by
duplicated detail.

Francesco Borromini,
Palazzo di Propaganda
Fide, Rome, 1662
Detail of door post:
concavity standing on
convexity.

to which Piranesi is the greatest contributor, was not mainly melancholic and death haunted, but an extravagant prompting to sensuous indulgence, notably in the mock ruins that decorate English landscape gardens. Through this curious focus on decay one imbibes the idea of fragmentary ancient remains as almost alive, sharing many features of the life of creatures and therefore inviting an intensity of response one does not usually associate with the insensible stone of architecture.

Some of the most interesting writing (by Hans Sedlmayr and others) about the lighter Rococo which the Baroque gently modulates into, argues that all its apparent frivolity and light-headedness is an unconscious attempt to fend off knowledge of ageing and death. So it introduces the cult of youth and sexual love in flight from Christian notions of sin and adult responsibility. So it is that the favoured colours are fresh pastels, undeepened by later, sadder experience, and the favourite activities are childish games, pastimes in more than one sense. Perhaps one can say the same about all exuberance, and even all art, that it is really about what it is not prepared to discuss or to face, that it is a kind of smokescreen hiding what cannot finally be hidden.

Frivolity aside, there is such a thing as mindless or unreflective exuberance of course, but the Baroque is full of instances of rapture attained by holding contradictions in tension rather than denying them, a demanding state of mind and feeling, not an easy or complacent one. Naive examples are among the most enjoyable, like the Mexican facades or *retablos* that have no idea how much is enough or too much, which turn Ionic columns into piles of luxurious, illogical detail, each one an independent principality that imagines itself infinite. In this strange and magical world, a modern observer can never be sure how many of the fantastic ideas spawned by these pseudo-architectural tapestries to attribute to the Indian carvers. Perhaps these teeming facades are simply archetypal cases of non-cohering collage, barrages of uncommunicating moments.

Contradictions held in deliberate suspension lie at the heart of Bernini's bravura pieces like the *Ecstasy of St Teresa* (1652) or the *Blessed Ludovica Albertoni* (1674), where violent energy and peaceful dissolution are present simultaneously in the same bodies. But it is preferable here to turn to the less obviously figural, more austere work of Borromini in the search for examples of thoughtful exuberance. Remarkably, in many of his buildings, like San Carlino (1638–41) at the beginning and Sant' Ivo (1642–60) near the end, a detailed narrative is translated entirely into architectural form; that is, into geometrical solids without simple avatars in ordinary reality. And in Borromini the thrill always comes from the discomfort of needing to solve a puzzle before one can take the next step. Why does the dome of Sant' Ivo twist and turn; twist and turn so much, in fact, that the whole idea of a dome is on the point of being lost? Why does the concave-sided pillar sit on an oval cylindrical base at the Propaganda Fide (1662)? Why, except that this discomfort is a stimulus to thought, and that the best thoughts arise from the exuberant variety that contradiction tolerated brings.

Of course in recent decades architects have gone much further than anyone could in the Baroque to produce anti-architectural effects in buildings that look as if they could fall down or come apart, like Frank Gehry's own house in Santa Monica (1977–8, revised 1993) caught in mid-explosion, or Rem Koolhaas' new CCTV in Beijing (2009), leaning and twisting as if it cannot possibly hold still. Of course, too, the more unlikely these illusions are, the more they send one back to the minds of their designers. As in the 17th century, the wildest contemporary forays are the starkest assertions of the power of human artifice, exactly the effect that many of the projectors thought they could avoid. Thus like the most vigorous Baroque works they create experiences whose visceral power does not last long except in uncomfortable oscillation with cerebral reflection that begins in the moments after the initial shock. It is up to the viewer or user to decide whether these designs are facile games indulged in simply because they are possible, or profound exposures of the contradictions always present in experience but unnoticed until someone like Borromini startles us into troubled appreciation. ∆

LET'S ROCK OVER BAROCK

Since the 17th century, Austria has been a stronghold of the Baroque. Here **Wolf D Prix** of Coop Himmelb(l)au recognises the deep pull of this cultural tradition in contemporary Austrian architecture, as it continues to endow its designers with an aptitude for spatial sequence and a tendency to prefer to design complex spaces over simplified boxes.

Julian Fors, Jan Gronkiewicz and Dominik Strzelec (Studio Prix, University of Applied Arts, Vienna), Chardach, New Levent Subcentre, Istanbul, 2008
Taking the ancient Grand Bazaar and Istanbul's *gecekondular* (informal urban dwellings) as its reference, the main goal of this student project was to create a building that could function as a new subcentre for the city's Central Business District, animated by a shopping mall designed according to the traditional way of trading and living in Istanbul and answering global networking tendencies. The complexity of the programme, its location in a highly dense area, and the very large total surface presented a number of challenges. Three different typical strategies were thus set up: one experimental concerning spatial geometry, one based on virtual social space networking, and one conventional urban strategy. The result is a new architectural typology.

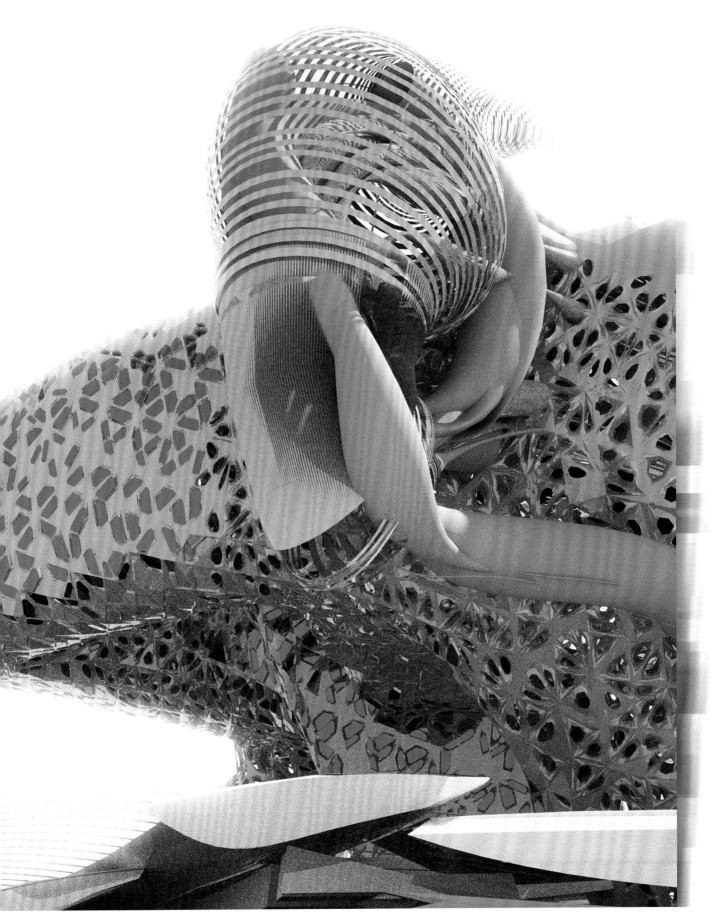

The dialectic between the 'tangible' and the 'abstract' is constituted by the feedback between models and the computer as a design tool. In this manner, an open system of interaction serves as the foundation for the development of a new formal architectural language.

The desire to celebrate space could be what constitutes a specific, shared, distinctive Austrian architecture. Young Austrian architects are showing that, for all their diversity, it is nonetheless possible to realise a unique quality in Austrian architecture: the architecture of the spatial sequence.

Although architecture must also be thought of in global terms, it is becoming increasingly important to develop the unmistakable uniqueness of an authentic architectural language, one that can be defined only in the context of a cultural background. We can embark upon the attempt to define, through their cultural roots, the world's architects who determine the architectural discussion at the moment. We can call the Dutch and the Swiss, in contrast to the Austrian space inventors, strict ,'diagram Calvinists'; a Gerrit Rietveld in Vienna is just as unthinkable as a Frederick Kiesler in Rotterdam. We can call Frank Gehry, Eric Owen Moss and Daniel Libeskind Cabbalists, and mystically describe their architecture as powerfully literate and eloquent. And Zaha Hadid's designs are clearly the spatial signs of Arabic calligraphies.

Yet in the search for the uniqueness of Austria's architecture, we constantly stumble upon the missing theoretical foundation that would allow an interpretation and stylisation of the architects' clearly evident qualities in such a way that a sharply contoured image appears of what might make Austrian architects distinguishable on the global scene: the desire to redefine built space.

Although this lack of a supporting theory might open up individual possibilities, the often acclaimed diversity – perhaps otherwise a sign of strength – is ultimately just the sum of lone warriors that opens the gates to international recognition for only a few Austrian architects.

Whereas in other countries young architects learn to ride the slipstream of their land's greatest names, in Austria we practice patricide. However, this patricide is not an act of liberation: it is simply an unruly defiance of tradition, a reflection of Austria's anti-intellectual stance that prevents a discursive confrontation with the innovative architectural qualities that risk being novel.

What madness to build immensely heavy domes and have them vanish under heavenly visions. In taking the desire for spatial design evident in Baroque structures as a starting point, a particular skill of Austrian architects becomes clear: designing complex space rather than the simplified box. From Fischer von Erlach to Rudolph M Schindler and Frederick Kiesler through to Hans Hollein, Walter Pichler, Raimund Abraham, Günther Domenig and Coop Himmelb(l)au, the buildings of these architects are structural evidence of the existence of a formal language that places Austrian architecture unmistakably on the global scene.

Consciously or unconsciously, in ways appropriate to their era, young architects follow the Baroque traces of spatial sequences and change them. There is still an Austrian tradition, as it were, which goes beyond the scattered battles of lone warriors: it is the shared desire to celebrate space.

Such tradition continues in education. In Studio Prix at the University of Applied Arts in Vienna, the budding architects not only discover how to develop ideas, but also how to argue in conceptual terms. They also learn to further develop, refine and celebrate their ideas in the wind tunnel of reality, not for the reality of clichés, but for the reality of possibilities. This is essential when the goal is to design complex space instead of simplifications of it. Students are taught to design this complex space on the basis of haptic models and to analytically classify it in plans and cross-sections.

The dialectic between the 'tangible' and the 'abstract' is constituted by the feedback between models and the computer as a design tool. In this manner, an open system of interaction serves as the foundation for the development of a new formal architectural language. The constant objective is always architecture on a 1:1 scale that represents more than the bare fulfilment of functions.

In the 2009 academic year, students were asked to design a high-rise in Vienna able to generate energy through exposure to contextual dynamic forces (wind, solar). The focus is on the overall geometry according to the energy concept and on the development of the building skin. The semester began with the analysis of given examples of fluid dynamics. Students simulated effects and phenomena through the use of digital simulation tools. As a transition from principle research to applied research, they then examined technologies that can transform dynamic movement into energy (heat, electricity) and sketched concepts of a proposal for a facade element that would use these principles. Based on their studies of dynamic forces, and the subsequent virtual and physical model studies, the students were able to begin work on the development of the high-rise building.

This example of a recent design studio programme illustrates young architects can be taught a strategy to augment seemingly wild ideas, first to developable concepts and finally to realistic architectural projects. It is important for architects to regain control of the architectural argument, whether the subject is conceptional or theoretical, technical or financial, in order to keep architecture a three-dimensional manifestation of culture, just as the works of our famous architectural predecessors did. Δ

'Rock over Barock: Young and Beautiful: 7+2' was a touring exhibition which was held at the Kunsthaus Mürzzuschlag in 2004, the Aedes Berlin in 2006, and the Venice Architecture Biennale in 2006. See Wolf D Prix and Thomas Kramer (eds), *ROCK over BAROCK*, SpringerWienNewYork (Vienna), 2006.

Damjan Minovski (Studio Prix, University of Applied
Arts, Vienna), Power Highrise, Vienna, 2009
The rigid shape of a high-rise slab is here transformed
by different layers of information processed from the
building's location. The information (wind speed and
resulting turbulences at the building surface, structural
load, sun exposure, etc) were stored in image formats and
filtered by pixel-based operations and techniques such as
erosion filters. In a continuous feedback loop of changing
parameters and results, the collected information
determines the final shape of the building.

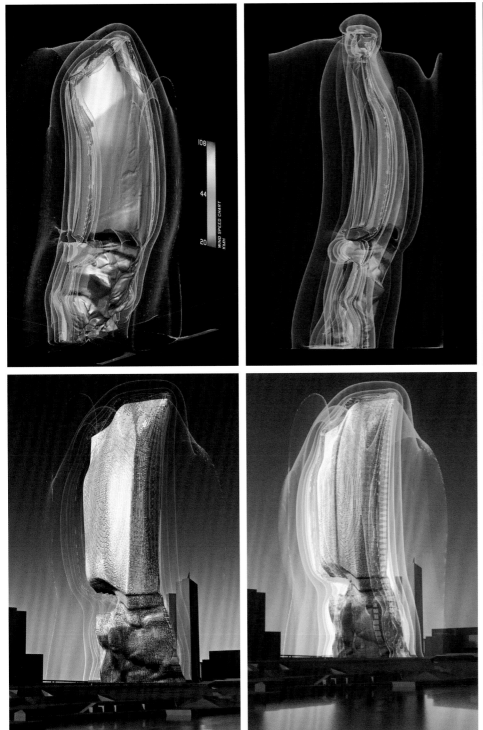
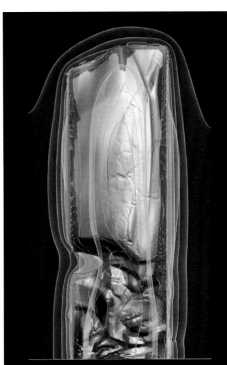

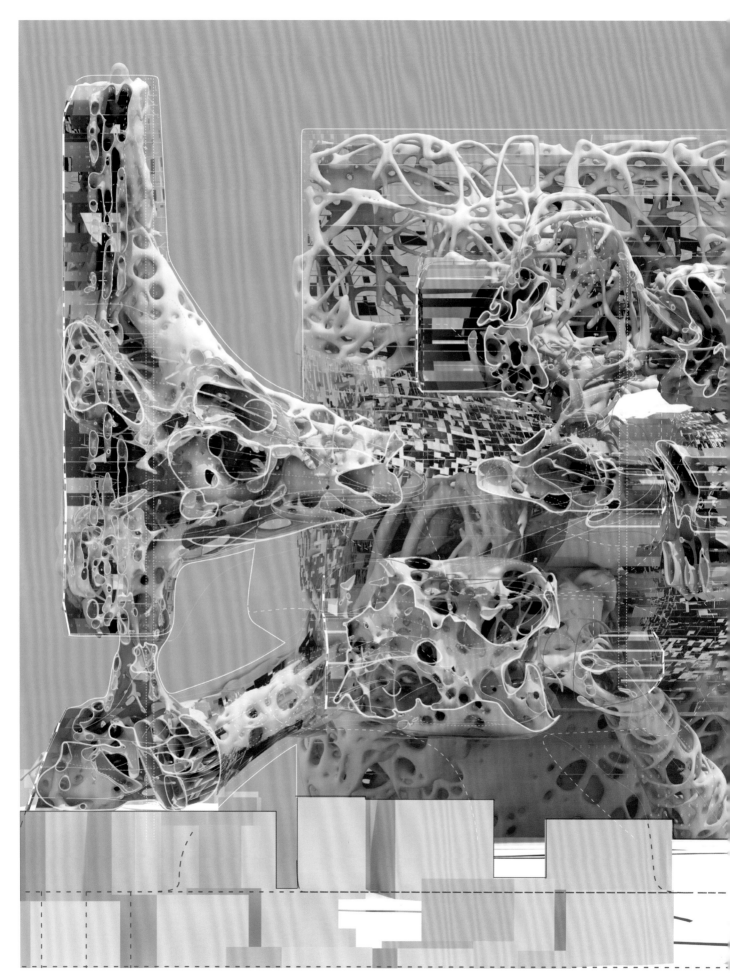

Vojislav Dzukic, Stefanie Theuretzbacher and Rupert Zallmann (Studio Prix, University of Applied Arts, Vienna), High Density, Levent, Istanbul, 2008
High-density shopping where goods and services are provided within an organism that grows through and around its surroundings, composed of living, office and hotel clusters. The clusters of functions are subdivided into modular units that are made up of structural and spatial components, such as partitions, floor slabs and facade elements. The parameters that define the formal and functional properties of the modules are driven by (most importantly) sun illumination, organisation of functions and viewpoints.

Rupert Zallmann (Studio Prix, University of Applied Arts, Vienna), Substitute Matrix, Wiener Eislaufverein, Vienna, 2009
The Substitute Matrix is a system that registers data (from the site and the given functional requirements) two-dimensionally into a spreadsheet where it is then analysed and reorganised. The format of the spreadsheet represents the undistorted and unrolled volume of the building. The processed data is transformed directly into spatial elements and located on the site. The driving parameters of the matrix for this specific 'case study' building, a multicomplex incorporating an ice-skating rink, wrestling arena, hotel, and retail and recreation facilities, are climate control, lighting, functional densities, structural properties and circulation requirements. Hence its appearance and spatial complexity is not designed, but depends merely on the overlay of different layers of variable numeric information.

Rupert Zallmann (Studio Prix, University of Applied Arts, Vienna), Substitute Matrix, Wiener Eislaufverein, Vienna, 2009

+54.00m

+40.00m

+20.00m

+7.50m

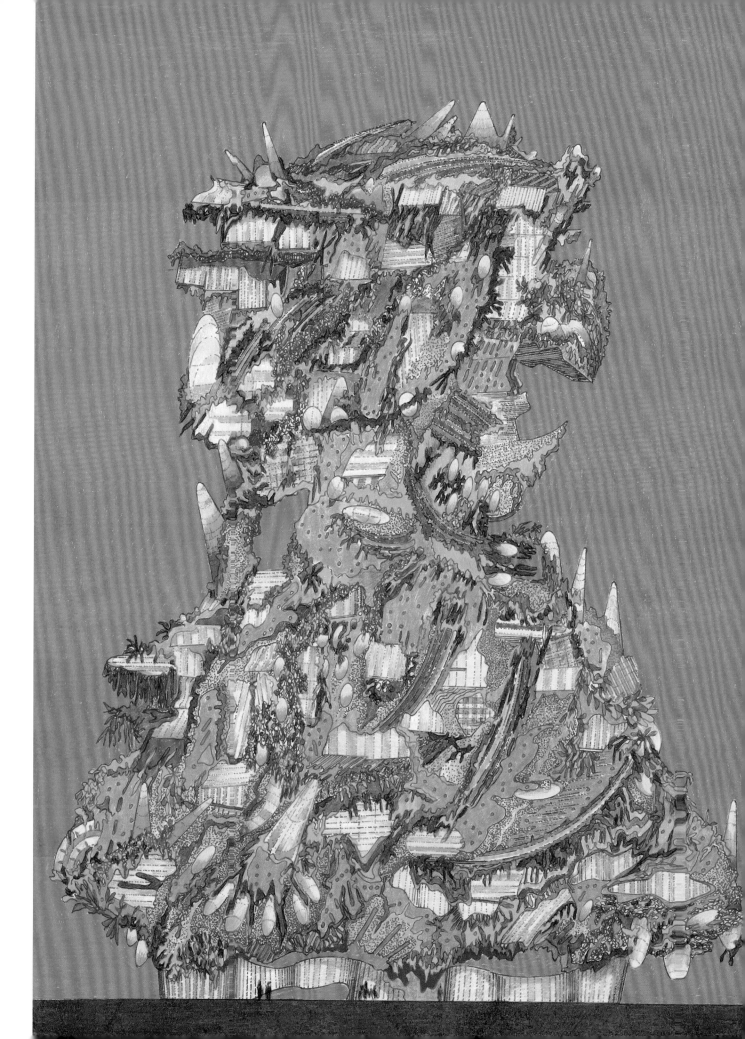

THE NEW DELFINA

Peter Cook eulogises the exuberant: he urges us to recognise its potential for release, as a true opportunity to let go creatively – and, in fact, to let it all 'rush out in a torrent'. In tandem, he redraws the Sheraton Delfina in Santa Monica from his hotel window, as an exuberant pile or liveable conglomeration of grotto-like spaces.

Architects should never get nervous about exuberance: it's wonderful. It's a great release. A great opportunity for funny bits and pieces that lurk around in the recesses of one's creative tank to burst forth.

'Letting it all hang out' is only one aspect. Letting it rush out in a torrent, unencumbered by pace, taste, hierarchy, chosen moment, arguable relevance, correctness, sustainability credentials – in fact, credentials of description – that's the trick.

Remarkably, some of the excretions that tumble out will have messages to be sent back to the more circumspect moments of designing and may contain the architectural equivalent of the 'riff' in music. Our dull creative landscape surely needs the occasional riff?

Anyway, sitting here in Santa Monica and looking out of our fifth-floor hotel window I see a shadowy lump in the near distance. It is the Sheraton Delfina on Pico and Fifth. We are very close to the ocean, and the marketing description for the Delfina asks you to 'enjoy a relaxed beach attitude and total comfort … plenty of room to work or relax … one-of-a-kind settings for events'. Yet it sits there as a grim, grey chunk. Santa Monica is, after all, the ultimate destination of those millions of opportunists or escapists who made it to the States, then made it to the West then (if lucky) made it to the Hollywood Hills, Malibu or (if they want both sea breeze and a bit of town life), to Santa Monica. Hordes of English, Austrian, German and Argentinian literary or design types headed there to chill out. Some of us still do.

So the slightly more exuberant pile (or is it a heap?) suggests a liveable-in conglomeration of suites, caves, boudoirs, pool houses, eyries, entertaining pads, private zoos, dells, knolls …. And not a few categories of space or room or conjunction for which my narrow mind is still wary of. (Dominated – despite itself – by the history of typologies as established by so many generations of technical universities and codified by Mr Neufert or the compilers of the *Metric Handbook*).

Enjoy ! ⌂

Marjan Colletti

ORNAMENTAL PORNAMENTATION

THE ABSTRACT AND THE EXUBERANT BODY OF ORNAMENTATION

In the last few years, the introduction of new digital software has enabled the exuberant articulation of ornate surfaces and volumes. **Marjan Colletti** looks beyond technical innovation and observes a two-fold conceptual tendency that he labels the 'ornaMental' and the 'pOrnamentation', differentiating between the first's inclination to create form through abstraction and the latter's potential for the figural through sensation.

Marjan Colletti, 3&1/2D The
POrnaMental One, 2009
Misshapen, blobby, exuberant
digital lofts formed only by an
array of circles.

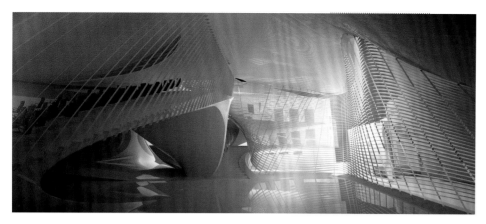

Damjan Iliev (DS10, University of Westminster),
Headquarters for the Organization of the Islamic
Conference (OIC), Istanbul, 2007–08
As the only international hub situated on two continents
simultaneously, Istanbul provides an extraordinary complex
cultural setting in terms of its social, ethnic/religious and
urban ambit. The project aims to integrate Istanbul's
rich historic past as a centre of trade and religion
with its increasing importance in worldwide politics.
It examines optical defocusing and cognitive illusions,
transparency and refraction, openness and veiling. Various
experiments challenge preconceived notions of visual
perception through the methods of reflection, refraction
and distortion. A series of isomorphic physical and digital
models construct optical illusions based on projected
geometries that visually alternate from various points.

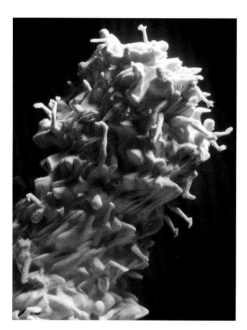

Yousef Al-Mehdari (Unit 20, Bartlett
School of Architecture, UCL), The
Descent, 2007–08
The collective body is the portrayal
of masses of bodies as a single
entity – be it a deliberate act of
representation or an accident of
interpretation. A sense of direction is
employed in order to suggest some
form of travel – in this case vertical
(hence the title). Chiaroscuro effects
are used to dramatise certain scenes
in the Descent, and to blur the
boundaries between the animate and
inanimate. Ultimately, the blending
of the body with its surroundings is
explored to understand the uses of
the figural ornament as a revived
mode of narrative.

The recent proliferation of digital techniques has brought an abrupt close to the seemingly enduring separation of tectonics and ornamentation in architecture. Small variations in software protocols and fabrication mechanics can result in the more or less exuberant articulation of ornate surfaces and volumes. Besides tooling systems and mechanics, one can also observe a twofold conceptual pursuit of such synthesis of digital ornamentation and tectonics, which can be termed the 'ornaMental' and 'pOrnamentation'. The first propels towards 'pure form' through abstraction, the latter towards the 'purely figural' through sensation.

Both these vectors are delineated in Gilles Deleuze's book *Francis Bacon: the Logic of Sensation*[1] and are described by the French philosopher as painting's chance to escape from the figurative in art. It can be argued that it is possible, within the digital domain of architecture, to trace a similar distancing from the digital design equivalent of the figurative in painting, the hyper-real rendering: the commercial illustration and depiction of architecture, that in all its sophistication and accuracy is not particularly intended to convey any theoretical, strategic or spatial properties. It is clear that such hyper-real simulations are per se 'hyper-fake'. Simulation replaces the real with a fictitious and artistic self-representation, a reiteration of its own – digital – properties and characteristics.[2] Architecture becomes a figuration of a hyper-fake simulacrum. It is only by avoiding it (as in Deleuze) that digital design can manage to articulate something purely original beyond the figurative rendering.

The OrnaMental
One way to distance CAD from the hyper-fake is by using the computer to perform an intellectual task that goes beyond simulation, representation and simulation of representation. Extrapolating from Bacon, it can be argued that the ornaMental is a digital, intrinsic cerebral expression of a synthetic, subjected and almost spiritual blurred code of abstraction. The 'digital' presumes a predominantly graphic mental system in order to construct a non-narrative and non-representational, yet mimetic,[3] digital code of ornamentation. The value of the ornaMental is that of aesthetics and application (understood as bodiless decoration, as software programming and as global applicability – as method). Without a body (or volume), the intellectual task of the ornaMental becomes the articulation of a mediated system for a possible symbolic structure or strategy for digitality. The ornaMental is elegant.

Islamic patternisation scripts, Modern art and geometry in particular provide the most likely reference material for this branch of contemporary digital design.

As known, Islamic architecture omits figuration and constructs a taxonomy of patterns and ornaments that express a basic tenet of Islam: not to be misled into an imaginary and idolatrous world. Ornamentation here is not mere decoration, it has an intellectual, mental, metaphysical bias. That the Middle East has experienced an urbanistic/architectural/financial boom has also well served such developments.

The abstract, immaterial, partly indeterminate nature of the visual arts in the early 20th century has also deeply inspired Modern, experimental architecture, initially in its non-figural 2-D graphic domain and recently in its 3-D software modelling environments. Abstraction equals ornament.

And a similar generative logic and morphological syntax is nowadays being

Yaojen Chuang (Unit 20, Bartlett School of
Architecture, UCL), Chronicles of a Cure, 2007–08
Chronicles of a Cure seeks to derive spatial
representations from the concept of an architecture
of moods. It posits a series of environments that
correspond and capture a sense of sacredness,
weightlessness, the disintegration of the boundaries
between the body and its surroundings along with
the spaces that reflect these saturated emotions
and the heightened senses. The design emphasises
the multiplicity of the sensory experience through
the spatial manipulation of perceptions and senses,
with the aim of promoting coherence of physical and
spiritual well-being.

embraced by parametric and scripted generative techniques to produce myriads of complex, patternised, ornamental topologies with more and more 'mental' attributes – albeit that the intellectual endeavour here usually drifts towards the generic and the dogmatic, and away from the phenomenological and the experiential. Here, ornament is flat, it has no body, and neither has architecture.

POrnamentation

Another way of avoiding the hyper-fake and hence the mimicked is by using the computer to perform a sensorial task. POrnamentation tends towards a digital, extrinsic corporeal impression of the isolated, deformed and dissipated forces of bodies. It is a purely sensual neural experience, of folded and distorted figures/shapes, that again is non-narrative and non-representational yet mimetic. The 'digital' here assumes a (porno)graphic explicit system to also construct digital mimesis. Ornament here is intrinsic to the exuberant dynamic form, to the (Baroque) deformation of convoluted lines and bodies – of *Gestalten*. Ornamentation here is not intellectual; pOrnamentation is to do with the visual consumption of the unequivocal athleticism and ergonomics of shapes and forms. In this instance, the values of ornament are not aesthetic and application, but aesthesis and performance. Performance is understood as task or, better, as meta-task (what is to be performed is the performing of a task), and as staging (the reality of the task is not identical to the real-life task). Without an intellectual structure (or strategy), the sensorial task of pOrnamentation is for the body/figure to become the ornament, or for the ornament to become the body. Hence

ornament and architecture are not flat but convoluted. POrnamentation is exuberant.

Such architectural repertoire is rooted in a different set of rather exuberant references and precedents; unusual or, rather, elusive to the mainstream digital theoretical discourse.

The Jain and Hindu Indian temples, or those of the Mayas, Incas and Aztecs: all of these architectures manifest a truly exuberant figural architectural ornamentation. Different to Islam, religion here promotes the creation and representation of a hyper-world of fetish and of simulacra, of eccentric avatars and sexual idols.

Or think of the Baroque and its passions, tormented visions and metaphysics; with all its magnificent figural, sensual, exuberant examples – Pietro da Cortona's *The Triumph of Divine Providence* (1633–9) or Gianlorenzo Bernini's *The Cathedra Petri* (1647–53) – that blur the dimensions of space (3-D) and time (4-D).

Some other pOrnamental features transpire in what may be called the contemporary 'cyber-streamlining' fever, sustained by an ever increasing amount of slick, fleshy, lofted furniture and building proposals – a very similar trend to that of the 'streamlining fever' of 1930s America.[4] The justification for the dynamic ornament is again very similar and to do with the manufacturing protocols: such machines and materials had then, and still have now, constraints that usually demand sharp and thin edges to be smoothed down.

The downside is that the ornaMental becomes decorative wallpaper, and that pOrnamentation may make you addictive and look always for more extreme formal contortions. As ever, albeit inherent to the thinking and tooling of digital – but not only

– architecture, ornament cannot be the only feature of architecture; after all, inhabitation is not an abstract thought, not mere fiction, and space is not only the modelling of forces, of friction. But then again, ornaMental pOrnamentation does not belong to the everyday, as much as Bacon or the Baroque do not consider themselves, in Waldemar Januszczak's words, 'perfectly formed, exquisite, delicate, so civilized, precious', but rather as the unperfect pearl that gives the name to style: 'blobby, exuberant, misshapen, difficult to handle, and exciting in a deformed kind of way'.[5] **Δ**

Notes
1. Gilles Deleuze, *Francis Bacon: The Logic of Sensation*, trans Daniel W Smith, Continuum (London) 2003, first published in France, 1981, p 2.
2. In fact, they are neither part of Realism as reality is not altered by the absence of reality effects, nor of Surrealism, which makes a clear distinction between what is real and what is imaginary. Instead, 'hyper-fake' renditions embed the unreal in its very own Baudrillardian 'real's hallucinatory resemblance to itself'. See Jean Baudrillard, 'Symbolic exchange and death', in Mark Poster (ed), *Jean Baudrillard: Selected Writings*, Polity Press (Cambridge), 1988, pp 119–48, 145.
3. 'Mimetic' here is derived from 'mimesis' (world-making) and not from 'mimicry' (simulation). This differentiation is crucial, as the latter pretends that CAD performs best when simulating something – usually reality, structure, etc. Digital mimesis, on the other hand, is understood as world-making, imagination and interpretation.
4. Once again there is no need for dynamic-looking, animate formed projects. However, this occurrence has a justification: smooth (Deleuzian) spaces, NURBS geometries and parametric models are described by complex, distinct entities that can be easily manufactured – milled, printed, thermoformed or cut – by specialist CAD/CAM machines. László Moholy-Nagy, *Vision in Motion*, Paul Theobald and Company (Chicago, IL), 1947, pp 53–4.
5. Waldemar Januszczak, 'Baroque! From St Peter's to St Paul's', BBC documentary, Episode 1, first broadcast on BBC4, 11 March 2009.

Neil Spiller

SURREALISTIC EXUBERANCE –
DARK MATTERS

For **Neil Spiller,** there is a current vacuum in much
of contemporary parametric design. It is devoid of
embodied cultural experience and character. Much
can be learnt by rediscovering the dark matter
of Baroque and Surrealistic art and architecture,
which through repressed eroticism optimised on the
simultaneous presence of the secular and the profane
– the heaving physicality of the everyday world and
the repressed strictures of the Catholic church.

Gianlorenzo Bernini, *Ecstasy of St Teresa***, Santa
Maria della Vittoria, Rome, 1647–52**
Bernini's great sculpture transfixes all who see
her. Is this sexual ecstasy dressed up as religious
ecstasy? This blurred distinction between the thrills
of the flesh and religious doctrine is critical to the
psychological hold the church has on some.

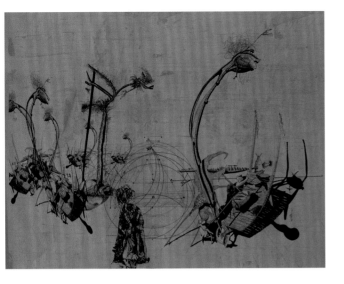

Neil Spiller, The Chapel of
the Twisted Christ, 2006
Drawing showing the
relationship between Christ,
vista and sculpture frontally.
The allegorical figure of St
Catherine is used to provide
scale and a nuance of the
rest of the chapel.

Many secular writers have interpreted the visions of St Teresa,
and particularly Bernini's great sculpture, *Ecstasy of St Teresa*,
at the Santa Maria della Vittoria church in Rome (1647–52), as
darkly erotic. The intention here is to explore this exuberant dark
eroticism and its poetic potential. It is also to point out that most
of our contemporary architecture has forsaken this dimension of
architectural discourse and its potential for exceptional spaces.

Churches are places of repressed sexual desire, fetishised
objects and peculiar rituals, which are redolent of bodily,
spiritual and mental supplication. Ethereal desire is deployed
to contain and dilute earthly psychosexual desire. Church
architecture moves the eye and soul upwards, inspiring a longing
for wider horizons of knowledge, but still some of this desire
for knowledge is carnal. The objects, reliefs and stained-glass
windows are corporeal, visceral and often bloody. The Surrealists
understood this strange concoction of paradoxes well. Much
Surrealist art bloomed out of exploiting the dichotomy of church
teaching and a heaving, amorous, secular world. St Teresa is
simultaneously emblematic of these two readings of 'ecstasy'.

According to Alberto Pérez-Gómez:

A building project ... has to be substantially completed
before construction can begin. In order to live up to
these imperatives and yet be capable of innovation, some
contemporary architects have sought to collapse 'theory'
and 'practice' in new 'algorithmic' processes of design
that avoid subjective 'judgement' and produce novelty
through instrumental mathematical operations. Made
possible by powerful computers and ingenious software,
the new algorithmic magic creates novelty without love,
resulting in short-lived seduction, typically without
concern for embodied cultural experience, character, and
appropriateness.[2]

Much avant-garde contemporary parametric design suffers from
this lack of love.

The term 'Cyberoque' is probably 10 years old. It was
predicated on the notion that the new virtual technologies
would blow life into architecture and we would head off to a
new architecture of billowing surfaces, voluptuous skins and
seductive invaginations. Indeed, the formal articulations that are

*I saw in his hand a long spear of gold and at the
Iron's point there seemed to be a little fire. He
appeared to me to be thrusting it at times into my
heart, and to pierce my very entrails; when he drew
it out, he seemed to draw them out also, and to
leave me all on fire with a great love of God. The
pain was so great, it made me moan, and yet so
surpassing was the sweetness of this excessive pain,
that I could not wish rid of it.*

St Teresa[1]

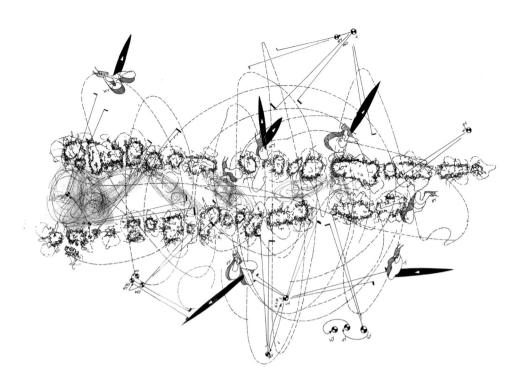

possible for the contemporary architect are much increased, albeit mostly in a familiar series of articulations begat by similar software applications. Much has been sacrificed to this formal necromancy and this includes properly articulated plans, expedient economic structural logics, and the exquisite dovetailing of form and programme.

Unfortunately all these tropes and trends lead us not to an architectural world of individual liberation, unleashed creativity and empowerment, but to one of ubiquity and a lack of self-critical engagement in the process of design and, most crucially of all, a lacuna of human communication through architecture that engages the human condition in all its myriad complexities and desires.

Communicating Vessels is an ongoing large and dense theoretical project that addresses some of the surreal possibilities of the new technologies in response to ideas of individuality, mnemonics, poetics, machinery and the history of art and architecture. The project is a mechanorgyistic 'pataphysical chunking engine' constructed out of desire, chance, poetry and Surrealist history. It is conceived as an alternative to contemporary digital architecture, yet it is digitally contemporary. It rejoices in fundamental natural imperatives and living technologies. Its teetering dynamics oscillate around a mythical island, half there, half not. It rides its metaphorical bicycle through the pantheon of art history and tosses itself happily into the dark crevices that are between and across poetic architectural desire.

The objects in the project occupy a vectorial space that is always shifting and unstable. Relationships change and symbolisms vacillate.

This is the English country garden of a heavy-metal Mad Hatter with dark Baroque sympathies. The epistemological distinction of plants, animals and machines is eroded. The conscious and the subconscious worlds are dallied with to create a psychosexual landscape that flirts with good and bad taste yet makes important observations and precedents for architecture and its systematic future. Elements explored in the light of these notions include: the entrance; the gate; the tree; the vista; the fountain; the sculpture; the bower; the gazebo; the artist's studio; the site plan; the seasons; the temple of repose; the chapel; the love seat; the laboratory; the dovecote; the shed.

Featured here is the Chapel of the Twisted Christ, a piece that seeks to subvert the chapel typology so that it becomes a celebration of the delight of chance, of the desire for exceptional difference and of the creative opportunities of the psychosexual paranoid–critical method.[3]

The chapel's meanings are manifold. It engages with St Teresa's two aspects of ecstasy and the paranoid-critical methodology utilised so effectively by Salvador Dalí and originated in Alfred Jarry's rereading of Albrecht Durer's woodcut of St Catherine in terms of her beheading. Another St Catherine (of Siena) bore stigmata. She is often depicted as receiving them from a church altar crucifix. The Twisted Christ writhes not to the preordained geometries of artistic suffering, but through the changing relationship between a vista and its orbiting sculpture determined by chance. So the Gothic sway of the Christ becomes the Gothic swerve. The swerve is one of Jarry's proto-Surrealistic declensions of his made-up 'pataphysics', a poetic conceit predicated on the particularity of the moment and the notion that everything is exceptional. So the chapel is a Chapel to Exceptions and the Desiring Swerve. It combines both holy and sexual imagery in direct contrast to the empty asexual husk of contemporary architecture. The laser damage to St Catherine's dress is further input data for other structures within the project.

We desire the exceptional, we want to be different, and we want all things to have a special relationship with us. We make our world by desiring within it. We should build our architecture with desire. **Ɖ**

Notes
1. St Teresa of Avila, Chapter XXIX 'Of Visions, The Graces Our Lord Bestowed on the Saint. The Answers Our Lord Gave Her for Those Who Tried Her', *Life of St Teresa of Jesus, of The Order of Our Lady of Carmel*, p 256. Online publication at Christian Classes Ethereal Library, http://www.ccel.org/ccel/teresa/life.viii.xxx.html, accessed 6 August 2009.
2. Alberto Pérez-Gómez, *Built Upon Love: Architectural Longing after Ethics and Aesthetics*, MIT Press (Cambridge, MA), 2006, p 28.
3. By 1930, Dalí was starting to develop his paranoid-critical method. He showed that an artist could obtain spectacular results by the controlled and lucid simulation of mental disease. Paranoia is an interpretative disorder with a rational basis which, if skilfully mastered by the painter, will allow him or her to reveal the double significance of things. The painter will act and think as if under the influence of a psychic disorder, while remaining fully aware of what is going on. The paranoid-critical method is most often psychosexual in its double images.

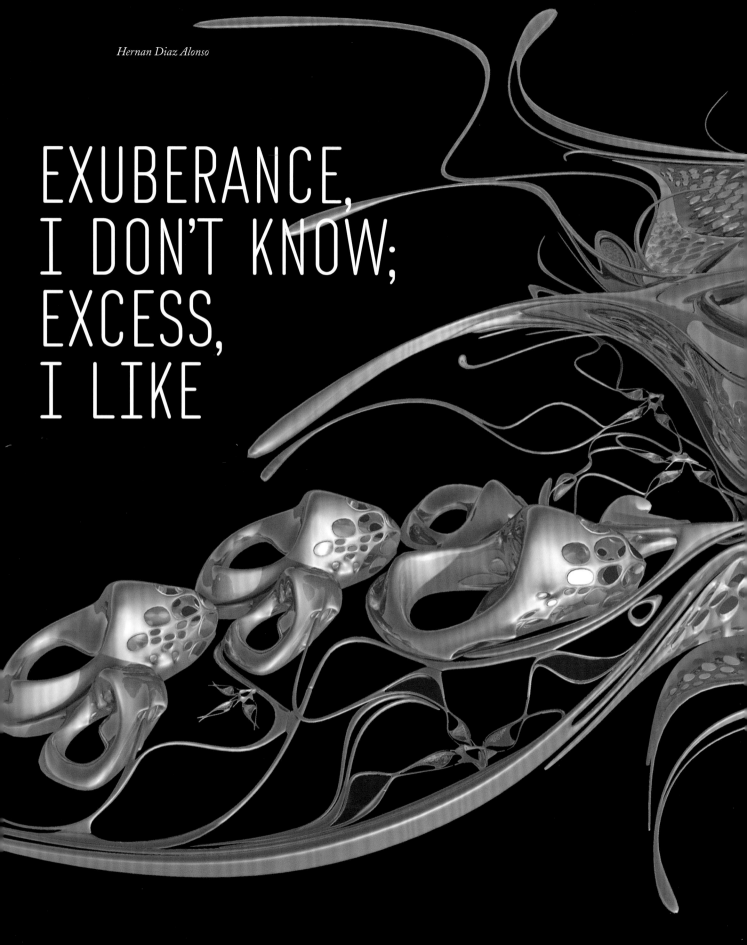

Hernan Diaz Alonso

EXUBERANCE,
I DON'T KNOW;
EXCESS,
I LIKE

Xefirotarch, Patagonia Museum Pavilion, Patagonia, Argentina, 2008–
Operates with the territory of affective arousement.

Hernan Diaz Alonso redefines 'excess' and 'exuberance' on his own terms. Fully *au fait* and comfortable with the excessive, he describes how in relation to his own work he views excess as more of a tendency or a logic, which sums up his approach; whereas he perceives the exuberant as removed from the design process and more like an 'adjective', an 'emerging quality' observed by others.

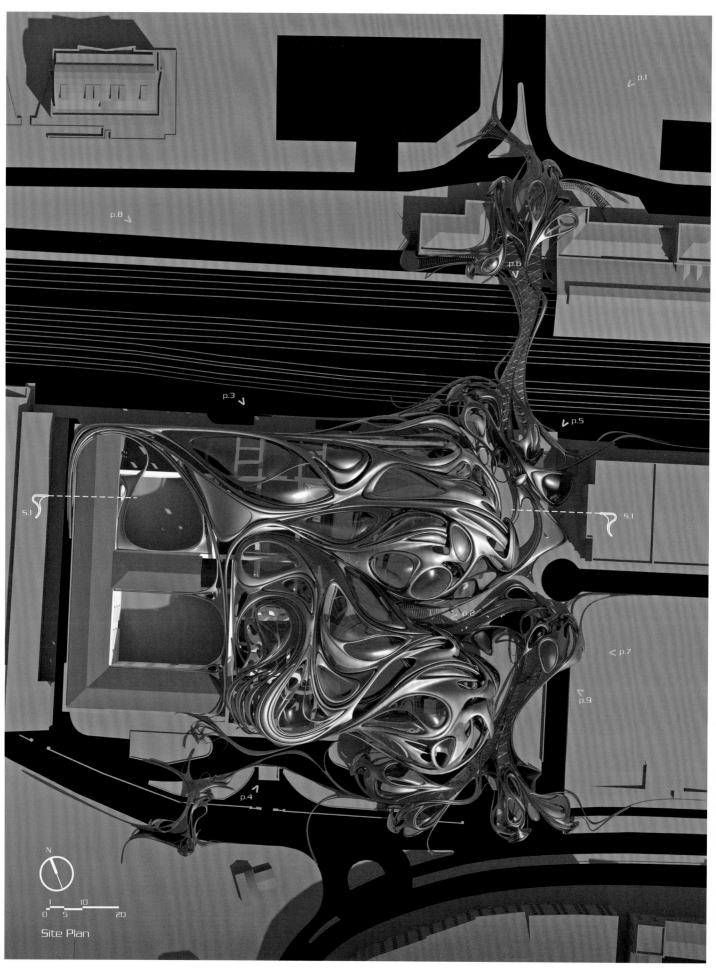

p.1

p.8

p.6

p.3

p.5

5.1   5.1

p.2

p.7

p.9

p.4

N

1   10
0   5   20

Site Plan

Xefirotarch, Tabakalera
Multimedia Museum, San
Sebastián, Spain, 2008
Operates with the genealogy
of cellular growth.

I have been trying to understand for some time whether there
is any difference between exuberance and excess, particularly
because I had been using the latter as a way to try to catalogue –
not necessarily explain – some of my recent work. I even named
my monograph like that.

It seems that there is (perhaps) not much if any difference.
What I think is useful is to define them as my own terms, and
I would say that 'exuberance' feels more like an adjective or
emerging quality, while I see my own 'excessive' tendencies as
more of a methodology or logic.

Below are some random notes in no particular order.
Please do not look in the dictionary to corroborate any of these
incoherent lines. I am sure they are all wrong.

Arousement/Excess

The first thing that comes to mind is that exuberance
relates to a condition of lust and desire, at least in terms
of setting an aesthetic agenda, and that is where I think it
became useful as a quality.

For discussions on the issue of form or formalism, the
word 'affect' has been at the centre as part of an ambition
to redefine the detachment of results from processes. At
least this has been the way that interests me.

In recent times – like in the last 48 hours – the
word 'arousement', or being aroused, is what I find more
proper in relation to the ambitions of the work that I
have been developing in the last two years. The word
'affect' seems to be a too general and abstract way to
define the behaviours of sensations that my formalism
implies. If anything should be clear by now, it is that
exuberance as an emergent condition is directly related
to affect, and so to put in simpler terms (my kind of
terms), excessive is the approach that I use to engender
arousement.

Mutation/Speciation

I am interested in the relationship between excessiveness
and speciation, and how species and systems of extreme
differentiation can produce a whole, but one which does
not necessarily claim homogeneity. Maybe that is one of
the points that I am trying to make: mutation can start to

define new territories for both excess and exuberance. This
new realm of exuberance, of mutating forms and excessive
allure, imply a new conception of beauty, one that does not
call upon the traditional understanding of the 'beautiful', but
instead one that seeks the aesthetically pleasing.

The Beautiful/The Horrific

If design was traditionally derived from an expertise of
form and proportion, even the mutation of design is also
an advanced state of that tradition. It cannot escape and is
thus an evolution of that tradition. Excessive topology then
becomes a tool of the highest control over, and manipulation
of, those formal strategies.

If traditional architecture needed to determine the
degree to which a particular project had achieved a state of
beauty, these excessive topologies explore the inverse of the
same register: the ugly and the horrific as material methods.
I see the ugly as a reversal of a more traditional beauty. The
horrific appears through encounter with that work, or as
part of some will to anguish.

Put another way, by rooting this topological design
paradigm within the confines of architecture's aim for
proportion and beauty, the ugly and horrific are the
necessary variations that allow for an escape towards a
spatial model of shocking presence.

Ultimately this is an aesthetic problem. In fact, I
do not aspire to inflicting a horrific feeling in people
through my architecture as an end in itself. What is really
interesting to me is the possibility of something horrific and
grotesque revealing a different kind of beauty and creating
a different kind of an effect and condition on the people
that experience my work. The result of the intensity of the
horrific is the appearance of some rare, unlikely new beauty.

Techniques/User Guide

Sometimes to explore this, the design is based on the
translation of what I understand, or imaging synthetic
biological techniques into formal-topological techniques,
for example creating basic taxonomies of a cell that generate
new species of formal behaviour. I do not see this basic
impulse as really new, but I go at it in a much less reverent

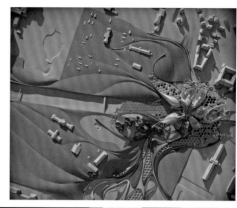

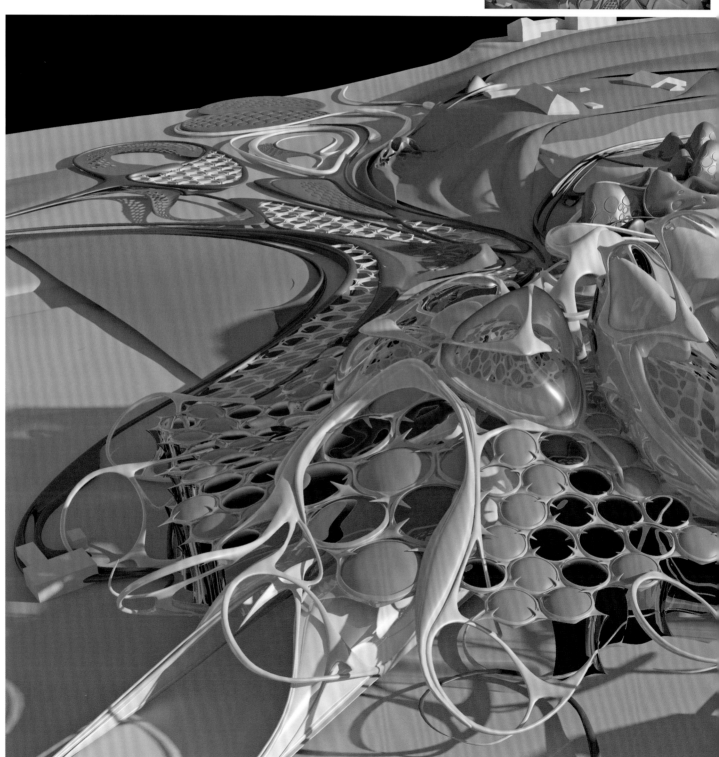

Xefirotarch, Warsaw Museum of
Polish History, Warsaw, 2009
Operates with the genealogy of
cellular growth.

Xefirotarch, Seroussi
Pavilion, Paris, 2007–08
left: Operates with the
terrritory of affective
arousement.

Xefirotarch, 'Lautner Redux',
Lautner Retospective,
Hammer Museum, Los
Angeles, 2008
below: Operates with the
realms of prosthetics.

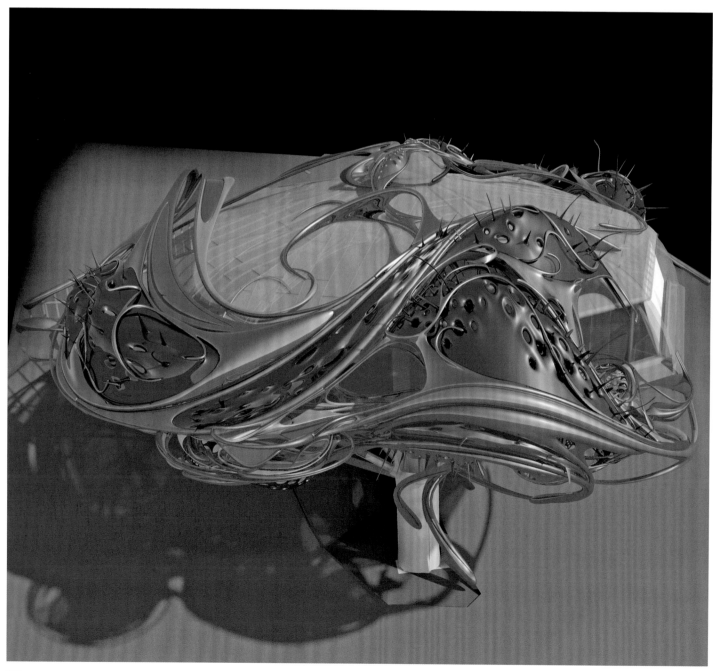

Xefirotarch, 'Pitch Black', MAK
Gallery, Vienna, 2007–08
Operates with the genealogy of
cellular growth and the horrific
as a new state of beauty.

way than most others have. To me the translations I am talking about from synthetic body to synthetic image are already at work. Michel Foucault's history of medicine is simultaneously a history of vision. The species becomes, in the modern regime of medical surveillance, an animated corpse, an assemblage of organs into which diagnoses are invested and installed. The inside becomes the outside. Or, more precisely, the insides become an interior structural condition to be understood in relation to another exterior structural condition; an epidermal membrane. There is nothing but excess all the way to the bones, which is itself another excess.

We imagine that architecture traditionally begins with a concept, an overall strategy or some kind of pre-meaning. I do not know if it ever really did as much as some people might say, but nevertheless it seems that the pursuit of exuberance can propose the possibility of form generation as a purposeful act in its own right that does not need a lot of justification.

As an extension of this interest, I think that in my work the excessive aesthetic as a method and a result focuses more specifically on the degree to which geometrical forms could be interpreted as an accumulative mutation, or as having latent affective potential, in their own right, all by themselves.

So again in comparison to traditional methods, there is irony in the fact that I am using mathematically precise systems (scripting within animation software) to produce monstrosities and grotesque decorative forms. The work is mutant, an autonomous life-form that is beyond human control. This is architecture intentionally without people or scale, but rather it is much more an obsession for variation, or an obsession to create different little formal species.

Image

As far as what comes out of all this, one of the critical shifts I focus on is the 'image', particularly the digital and digital cinematic image, as the main vehicle for the production of form. Design always concerns a translation between forms and formats of image. More

than 'textuality' or even 'iconography', in a lot of ways, its very form is a secondary function of how it performs as an image. Perhaps some might see this as a triumph of superficiality over depth, and they are not totally wrong. But the surface – the superfice? – is very complex. As it becomes more so, it is also an intensification of the projective and fictive logics of design, and of its technical ability to mobilise a social imagination and with it a series of potential futures. I see this as a real demand that society makes on architects as producers of a certain type of (architectural) content in the form of images of what things might be like next year.

Architecture is never displayed innocently. Any encounter with the work is framed by multiple determining contexts – political, sensual and spatial – that productively contaminate the moment of reception. And that is where any formal autonomy ends, and I am fine with that. That is not the part I am obsessive about. In this, the architecture's own highly charged perspective on the affects-ambiences – even especially site-specific works – becomes an invitation to visitors to trust their instincts, and to enjoy adventurously the works that they find. But it is up to them. Once people start consuming the architecture it is out of my hands.

Epilogue

Architecture is sort of a game, and it should be more so. I think it would be more powerful if it took play more seriously. I think that kind of a childish attitude towards working is important. We should validate the notion of fun and play. Children play games seriously, and most of the time they have an exuberance that we can only aspire to achieve. ∆

Notes
A very important part of this nonsense is the by-product of multiple conversations and long-term collaboration with Benjamin H Bratton, to whom I am eternally grateful.
1. Mick Jagger and Keith Richards, Lyrics from 'Rocks Off', opening track of the 1972 album *Exile on Main Street* (Atlantic Records/Rolling Stones).

Tom Wiscombe

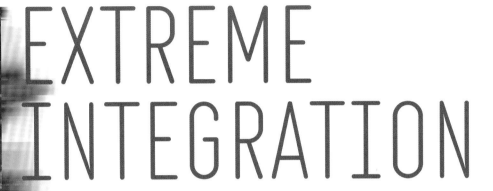

EXTREME
INTEGRATION

Tom Wiscombe advances an argument for
an architecture of 'extreme integration', where
the sanctity of the single surface responsible
solely for affect is challenged by multilayered
and multidimensional built surfaces. The new
species of architecture is 'robust enough to be
both formally and technologically innovative',
replacing a mechanistic model with a biological
jungle ecology of messiness and excess.

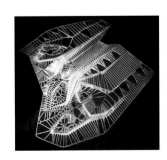

In Terry Gilliam's 1985 film *Brazil*, there is an unforgettable scene where Robert De Niro, a guerrilla air-conditioning repairman, responds to an urgent call for help from a sweating man. He has intercepted a call directed to the totalitarian state parodied in the film, and drops in out of nowhere to assist. De Niro removes a standardised interior panel from a wall, and mechanical systems behind literally pour out on to the floor in a shower of sparks and feeble pulsations. As he makes illegal repairs to the jumble of tubes and wires and ducts, he reveals his motivation: 'I came into this game for the action, the excitement, going anywhere. I travel light, get in, get out, wherever there's trouble.'

Brazil depicts a dystopian world in decline characterised by failing infrastructure and decadent culture. This scene in particular speaks to architecture: it takes place at the threshold between the extended visible world and the intensive technological systems and forces that underlie it. These realms are alternately at odds with, or effects of, one another: one is dysfunctional while the other is desperately keeping up appearances. De Niro's guerrilla operative is the unlikely agent of change.

Infrastructure and its relationship with the superficial has long been a point of productive contention in architecture. This history has been marked by two radically different sensibilities, one concerned exclusively with the visible realm, stuffing structure and building services into the spaces between walls and behind ceilings, and the other a modern rationalist desire to express or represent technology for its own sake. It is a tired dance in which both partners, Postmodernism and Structural Expressionism, have run their course but continue to appear on our skylines. With *Architecture of the Well-tempered Environment* (1969), Reyner Banham was one of the first to suggest that the history of building infrastructure in architecture is characterised by general neglect simultaneously manifested in the repression of environmental systems and an assumption of the primacy of structure in determining form. While problematic for its humanist underpinnings, his argument that retooling the relation of form, structure and lowly mechanical services can be generative in terms of design is intriguing and, to a great extent, still unexplored territory.[1]

Going one step further, assuming separation between the realms of building infrastructure and affect may be similarly unproductive. As interest in single-surface and topological projects wanes in contemporary digital design, there arises the possibility to think about surfaces not as abstract, endless and of zero-thickness, but as spaces of variable thickness, embedded and laced with structural, HVAC, plumbing and lighting systems. Once the sanctity of the surface as an independent agent exclusively responsible for affect is challenged, other logics and systems can begin to operate in a space that opens up between performance and sensation, infrastructure and ornament.

This is architecture of extreme integration, of nuanced transgressions of the extensive and intensive, of dipping in and out of *poché* space, pushing up against architectural surfaces, and reconstituting them in a more complex way. *Poché* becomes vivid, active space rather than blackened solids of classical architectural representation. The hung ceiling, one of the least examined *poché* spaces, must also be attended to in terms of its repressive function as well as its thinness. Moreover, a rethinking of the problem of standardised fixtures in ceilings and walls is long overdue, in the sense that the interface between systems and surfaces can be more productive.

Imagine instead the potentials of surface delaminations, embedded hollows, structural pleating, bundled micro-capillary systems and deep relief, where the iconography of technology and infrastructure dissolves as they are woven into architectural form.

Jungle Style

This is not an argument for a new techno-Functionalism, nor an endorsement of the neo-Baroque; rather, it is projecting a middle ground where architectural species are robust enough to be both formally and technologically innovative. The lens used is biology, a field often incorrectly cited by neo-Functionalists as a model for efficient architecture, and in particular so-called 'green' architecture. The thing about the biological world that resonates and fascinates is its seemingly limitless ability to generate excess; that is, exotic features and behaviours that are untraceable to any particular function. Biology obfuscates as much as it expresses: although it is possible to make generalisations about particular biological features and their performance, it is

EMERGENT, Thermo-strut, 2009
Prototype nesting a steel armature and a hydronic thermal system within a fibre-composite shell. Systems are discrete, but interlaced in a nuanced way.

EMERGENT, Tracery Glass, 2009
A new kind of stained glass combining gauzy colour and translucency effects with environmental systems such as solar PV, solar thermal and radiant cooling.

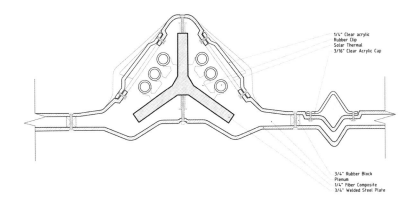

1/4" Clear acrylic
Rubber Clip
Solar Thermal
3/16" Clear Acrylic Cap

3/4" Rubber Block
Plenum
1/4" Fiber Composite
3/4" Welded Steel Plate

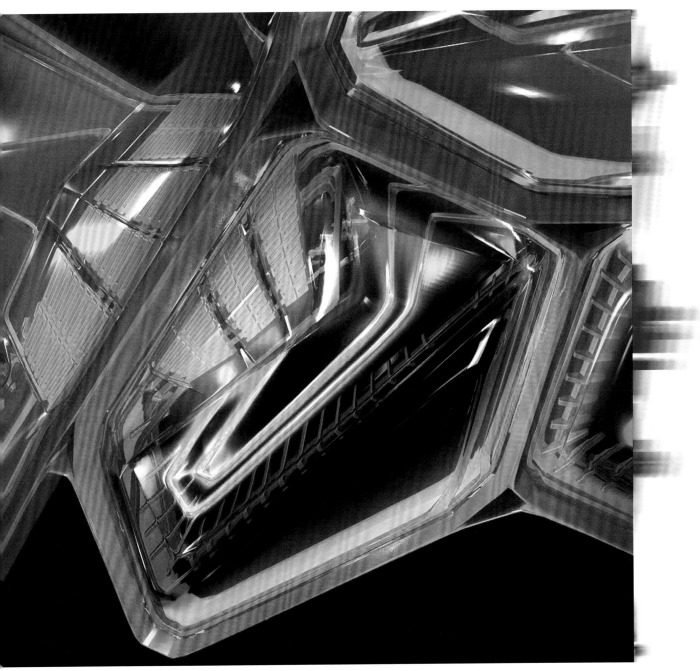

impossible to untangle with certainty the complex combinations of morphological features and behaviours of individual creatures or ecosystems. The deeper you look at organisms, the more the messiness of biology is revealed, and the more it becomes clear that it is inadequate to compare biology, which is about imperfect points of departure, adaptation, opportunism and emergence, with the field of engineering, which is very often lived as a reductive problem-solving routine.

It is doubtful, for example, that a jungle ecology could be 'engineered'. A jungle is too integrated. Jungles are always evolving based on local synergies between non-optimal conditions, material properties and adaptive behaviours. Indeed, the mantra of 'optimisation' has become a mental block for engineers and their profession at large because it assumes a single optimum condition rather than a multi-optimal ecology. A case in point is the *oeuvre* of Frei Otto, which has been instrumental in relating material distribution to form, but which is increasingly being used by others to promote 'minima' at the expense of messier biological models.

Getting to the space of multi-optimums, indeed of 'massive parallelism', however, is not as simple as adding more optimised systems on top of one another. It requires difference of kind rather than degree. The key, as with biological species and ecologies, is the active feedback loop that produces mutations and local inefficiencies that only later are revealed for their advantages. If a beam becomes a luminous pleat that can also move air, it may not result in the most efficient beam or duct or lighting system, but it will do work, and more importantly, it has the potential to produce nuanced jungle-style architectural effects. This is, to be clear, not an issue of engineering, but rather of design.

Consider the agamid lizard from Australia, whose skin exhibits several interwoven features – deep relief, micro-patterning, and colour variegation. Not all of these features are legible in terms of their performative values. It turns out that the deep grooves in the skin conduct water from the lizard's back all the way into its mouth, so it never has to drink. However, this function is obfuscated by other salient features of less obvious purpose and their combined visual effect. Excesses and messy overlaps of form and function allow multiple types of work to be done, from structural to environmental to ornamental.

Airflow, Fluid Flow and Glow

It is time to replace outmoded terms like 'building services' and 'mechanical systems' once and for all. Something servile will always be repressed, and repression will always impede experimentation in the realm of extreme integration. The notion of the mechanical brings us back to the industrial paradigm, rooted in a pre-networked world. And lighting design has become little more than a fixture-shopping experience. For now, maybe we can refer to these marginalised techno-systems in a more refreshing way as 'airflow', 'fluid flow' and 'glow'.

Beyond the prosaics of plumbing, fluids are on the cusp of having a huge impact on building design for two reasons: first, water carries thermal energy much better than air; second, fluid system applications are blooming into illumination, biofuel generation, architectural hydroponics, greywater distillation and so on. To frame this new sensibility, it is useful to think of fluids in terms of vascular systems, integrated networks characterised by bundling and weaving, micro-capillary systems, and also secondary emergent effects such as structural performance and heliotropism in plant stalks.

Aerodynamics, as well a fluid mechanics, is also open territory. Once you table the idea that air must be ducted into hermetically sealed spaces from a central source, you are free to consider the true complexity and possibilities of modulating laminar and turbulent flows, capitalising on natural aerodynamic behaviours triggered by thermal differentials, creating microclimates and buffer zones, and generally reconsidering environmental thresholds as design opportunities rather than as problems to be solved.

And 'glow', used as a verb, removes illumination from association with standardised fixtures. Glow denotes emanation from within, from behind, from unseen and unexpected sources, and therefore can be associated with thresholds between surfaces and systems in nuanced, ambient ways. All of this is most interesting in terms of crossovers and becomings, the point at which beams become ducts, where airflow and fluid flow are laced together into vascular arrays, or when colour features begin to co-evolve with structural features.

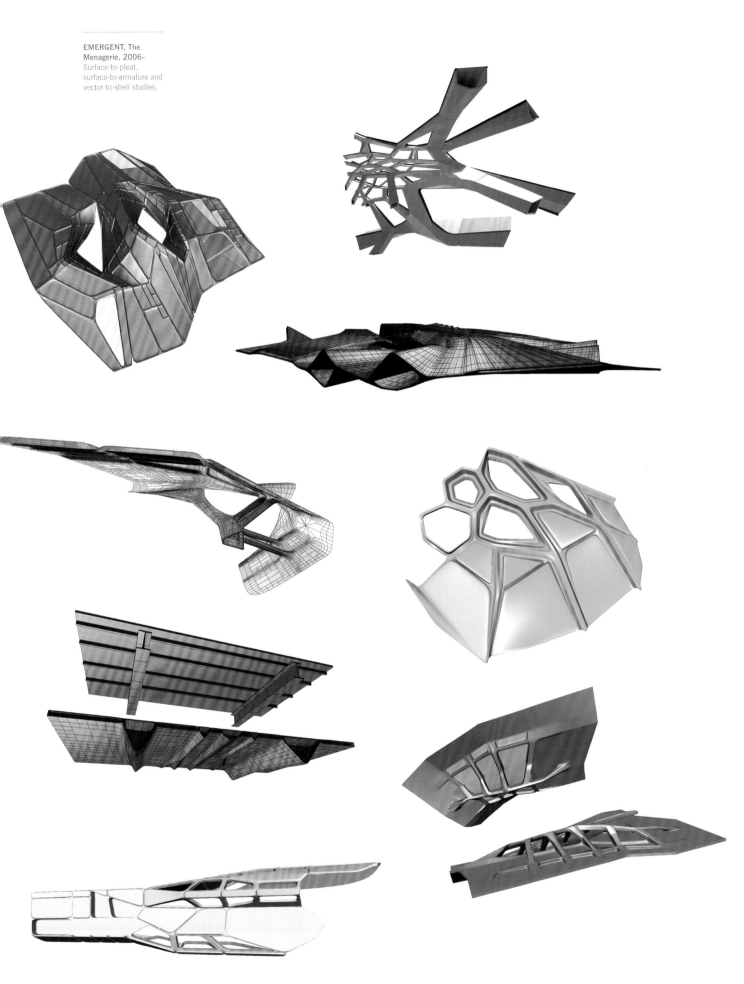

EMERGENT, The
Menagerie, 2006–
Surface-to-pleat,
surface-to-armature and
vector-to-shell studies.

EMERGENT, Flower Street BioReactor,
Los Angeles, California, 2009
below: The project is an aquarium-like
bioreactor inserted into the facade of
an existing building, which contains
algae colonies that produce oil
through photosynthesis. It features a
self-regulating growth system invented
by OriginOil, where tuned LED lights
dynamically vary in colour and intensity
according to the developmental needs
of the algae. This system is powered
by a solar array that winds up into the
branches of an adjacent tree, jungle style.

EMERGENT, Guiyang Office Tower,
Guiyang, China, 2008
right and opposite: The aim of
this project, based on hybridising
structural, mechanical and lighting
systems, was to avoid expressing the
literal image of technology in favour of
ambient atmospheric effects. Super-
columns become hybrid ducts, while
a pattern of micro-pleats runs along
surfaces, housing a heat-exchange
system for cooling. At night, the beam
ducts glow from behind the glass
skin, creating elegant colour effects
and gauzy silhouettes.

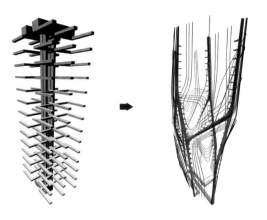

**EMERGENT, Taipei Performing Arts
Center, Taipei, Taiwan, 2008**
Three theatres are here interwoven
by way of an elevated concourse. The
concourse is characterised by mega-
armatures and micro-pleats, which
operate simultaneously as circulation,
structure, mechanical systems and
ornament. Deep spaces allow views
out into the city through gradients of
pattern and colour.

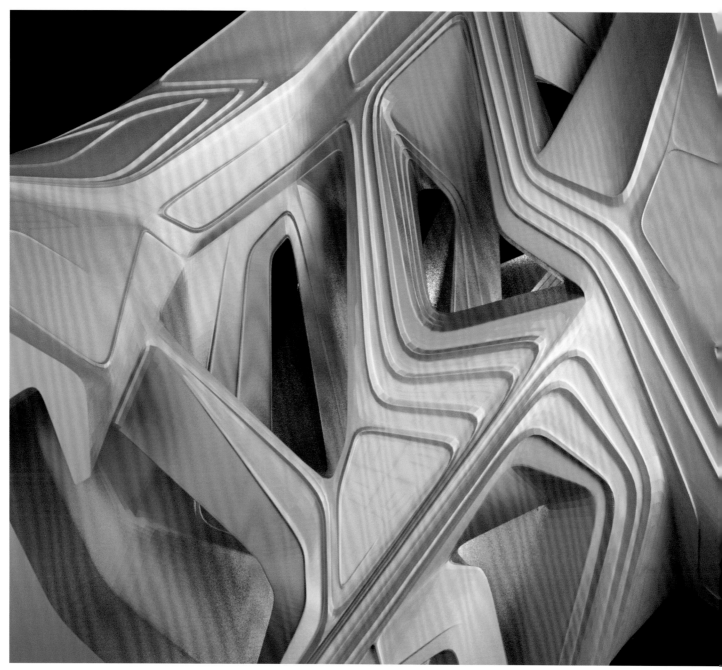

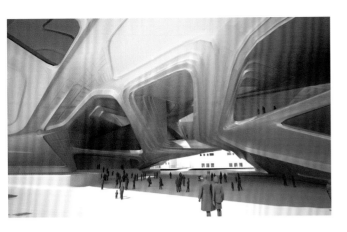

Surface-to-Strand Geometries

EMERGENT is currently exploring geometries that allow moving beyond both duality of frame-and-skin characterised by discrete systems and the 1990s topological project characterised by homogeneous smoothness and lack of articulation of systems. 'Surface-to-strand geometry' allows for both surface and strand behaviour as well as everything in between. One in-between geometry is a pleat, which is a becoming-strand of a surface. Surface-to-strand geometry is inherently useful in negotiating the realm of surface affect and infrastructural pathways. Its syntax enables radical shifts from beam to membrane, from bending to shell behaviour, from capillary to bundled structure. Some of the specific types currently in play are surface-to-pleat, surface-to-armature, relief-to-aperture, bundle-to-bramble, vector-to-shell, beam-to-membrane (beam-branes) and double delaminations.

To this end, the office has established a geometry dump, the Menagerie, that contains hundreds of surface-to-strand species. It is a well for projects. As some species are discarded, others take their place. Often, features of one species are combined with those of another, and a third species with novel characteristics emerges. So the language evolves.

The design process at EMERGENT often begins with the design of a prototype, a 'chunk', rather than thinking about the whole. Chunks consist of a set of features with a particular range of behaviour and a specific aesthetic sensibility. They are evaluated simultaneously for their quantitative and qualitative features; neither takes precedence all of the time. These prototypes have no fixed scale and their agency is deliberately left vague to allow for flexibility and chance in their incorporation within a building project. Importantly, they are not cells or agents that aggregate into scripted swarms, nor are they processed though a parametric gradient routine or 'blend-shaped' into a visual whole. They are not parts to be repeated or varied in an array – a characteristic of false emergence; rather, they are fragments of a whole that does not yet exist and cannot be predicted.

From Layers to Chunks

Designing in chunks instead of layers also reveals EMERGENT's wider interest in building in chunks rather than layers.

Building in chunks means that envelope, structure, HVAC, lighting and other embedded building systems can be delivered to the site as a composite assembly. This is both a new and an old idea: prefabrication gave architecture access to the industrial processes of the postwar era, but its potential was limited by its assumption of layers. Frames or panels were unitised and mass-produced – for example in the work of Charles and Ray Eames or Jean Prouvé – but never integrated as massively parallel, three-dimensional chunks. However, the architecture, engineering and construction industry is on the cusp of a sea change, especially with the advent of computer-controlled machining, a growing interest in composite materials, and the recent coming online of global fabrication networks.

While much of the building industry, especially in the US, remains balkanised and comfortable with layer thinking, subtle transformations are beginning to occur. One example is how technology transfers from the automotive and aerospace industries, predicated on integrative thinking, are flourishing. Likewise, the rush towards energy efficiency has resulted in an interest in embedding energy-saving and energy-generating systems into architectural assemblies.

Curiously, the advent of building information modelling (BIM) in recent years, while spurious as a design tool, has increased awareness of coordinating building systems and has finally forced structure, skin, airflow, fluid flow and lighting to be compiled in a single, three-dimensional environment. Nevertheless, coordination is false integration; a jungle ecology is not simply coordinated. BIM is deeply invested in the paradigm of layers in architecture, where components are standard and systems are rational and can always be disentangled. As a problem-solving tool, BIM is certainly capable of reducing collisions between systems – beneficial to developers and builders in terms of risk and cost, but ultimately unrelated to architectural design culture.

Extreme integration ultimately depends on messiness, excess and jungle thinking. It opens up a fertile, lush territory between extreme contemporary agendas that bias either effects or efficiency, culture or science, surface or vector. ⚠

Note
1. Reyner Banham, *Architecture of the Well-tempered Environment,* The Architectural Press (London/The University of Chicago Press, Chicago, IL), 1969, pp 11–17.

*Kjetil Trædal Thorsen and
Robert Greenwood*

RELYING ON INTERDEPENDENCIES
SNØHETTA IN THE MIDDLE EAST

**Kjetil Trædal Thorsen and Robert Greenwood of
Snøhetta** describe how opportunities to build multicultural
programmed buildings in the Middle East have opened
up the possibilities of developing a new iconography for a
new building type, embedded in the emotional translation
of a rich iconographic and decorative tradition; an ongoing
dialogue with the clients and users; and a Middle Eastern
preference to define the present by looking to the future.

Snøhetta, King Adbulaziz Center for Knowledge
and Culture, Dhahran, Saudi Arabia, 2009
The outer skin of the pebbles is given a
reflective surface of stainless steel. In front of
the glass the steel tubes are flattened to provide
effective sun-shading and allow users to enjoy
the magnificent view.

Multicultural programmed buildings tend to increase the complexity not only of each function represented and their internal relationships, but also of the overall conceptual complexity compared to monofunctional buildings. Unlike the opera house, the theatre, the cinema, the museum or the concert house, these new structures need to reinvent themselves not only in shape, but, more essentially, in function.

Like racehorses with eight legs, this multicomplexity is of an unknown kind. It may not be oversimplified or reduced in its expression, and represents the ism-free, pluralist, postindustrial thinking of countries not relying on their past as the final recourse for future development.

Once these countries get to grips with their cultural development, we will see architectures of new aesthetic and contextual content overriding preconceptions of the intellectual elite in Europe and the US. A wider definition of architecture, more open and performative in its connection to its users, environmentally intelligent, generating public ownership and social sensitivity might be the result. That is, if architects are able to act within the spirit of cooperation and dialogue alongside contemporary values without compromising long-term qualities or architectural integrity.

In many of Snøhetta's projects currently under development in the Middle East, be it in the United Arab Emirates or Saudi Arabia, the desert defines a primary plane of reference. Not unlike the oceans, these vast sand surfaces determine the width of the horizon and the size of the sky above. But however culturally significant to the Arab society and to the nomadic and Bedouin tradition, the desert is still hopelessly romanticised by Western interpretations.

Architects may use the lack of archetypical forms and historical architectures as defined within the development of the urban Western world, as well as the historic lack of imagery in Islamic art, to avoid superficial Westernisation of aesthetics. Solutions may rather be found in the emotional translations of a rich iconographic and decorative tradition. When processing these sources of inspiration architectural projects may turn into dialectic concepts and interpretations, where intellectual content can be discussed throughout the whole design process.

Interestingly, the possibility of working with unknown building typologies in the Middle East region does not seem particularly exuberant in the context in which they are being discussed, but rather intuitively normal and pragmatic with a hint of a very positive naivety. This of course is in great contrast with Europe's loss of naivety or, rather, its fear of the same. And while Europe is using its history as reference to all contemporary things, and the collective experiences of possible and not possible to limit experimental approaches, Middle Eastern societies prefer to look to a possible future to define their present.

Snøhetta is today involved in three major projects in Saudi Arabia: the King Abdulaziz Center for Knowledge and Culture for Saudi Aramco in Dharan, and the Dialogue Centre and the Library to the Holy Mosque, both in Makkah. The practice has here committed itself to exploring and developing architectures of high contextual, functional and aesthetic qualities. The content of each project touches deeply upon the current movement of cultural and social development in Saudi Arabia, initiated by forces looking for value-added changes within a population of which more than 40 per cent is under the age of 17. In addition, Saudi Arabia has a significant number of highly educated but, still typical of this society, unemployed young women, who have a strong interest in the cultural development of their society and are today an influential force in this endeavour.

The cultural differences witnessed during the development of Snøhetta's projects in Saudi Arabia have been outnumbered by the intellectual similarities experienced through meetings and discussions. Based on conversations relating to the generic human conditions of action and perception, levels of understanding have become solid and real. While trying to incorporate the best ideas of our Western democracies into a locally based evolution of wider knowledge, tolerance and cultural awareness, Snøhetta believes that architecture is one of the many important tools necessary to create a better future. This hypothesis relies on the brain as the essential creator of possible futures. The so-called 'mirror neurons' in the human brain are in charge of the influence of action on perception and vice versa. They control our ability to imitate, a prerequisite for learning and developing skills. Repetitive action leads to specific perception, and changes in repetitive action lead to changed perception. Architecture is action.

Snøhetta, Ras Al Khaimah Gateway, Ras
Al Khaimah, United Arab Emirates, 2009
Horizontality and verticality are combined
here into one flowing gesture, suggestive of
new building typologies that do not respond
to the more traditional archetypes of tower
and podium. These forms are instead
responding to a complex multifunctional
content and the shifting context of the
Bedouin landscape.

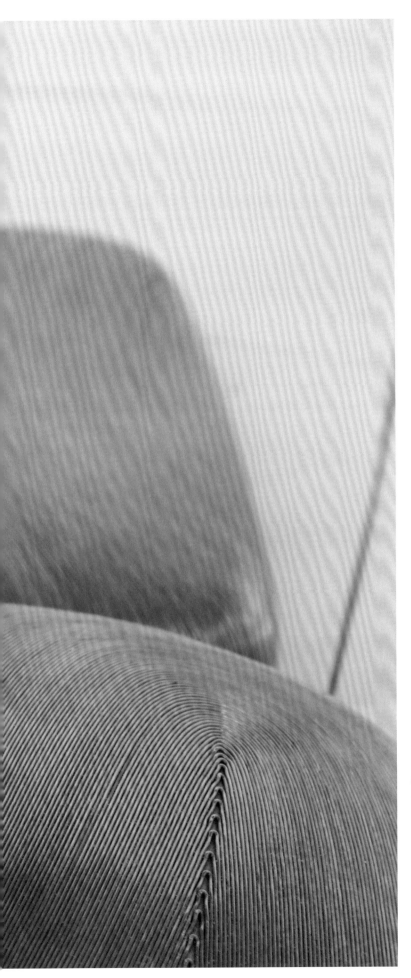

Model showing the keystone element and tubing lines of the outer skin. The lines enhance the definition of the shapes and animate the pebbles as the sun moves across the sky.

The building is wrapped by spiralling stainless-steel pipes providing both shade and ventilation for the insulated walls behind. In addition, the pipes will utilise the surface heat of up to 80°C (176°F) for energy production. With such surface temperatures, the pebbles will start to blur their edges creating a visual experience similar to air mirages.

Model view showing the Great Hall exhibition centre in the foreground, and the library, keystone, tower and auditorium from left to right in background. The shape of the main opening of each pebble defines the shape of the first steel tube; the rest of the tubes are offsets on the surface in even increments until they cover the entire surface. This forms a self-generating pattern driven only by the shape of the main opening and the shape of the pebble.

Snøhetta, King Abdulaziz Center
for Knowledge and Culture,
Dhahran, Saudi Arabia, 2009
Each element of the building
is given its own discrete and
recognisable form as a 'pebble'.
However, these individual pieces are
put together in such a manner that
at the same time they visually and
physically support each other.

The King Abdulaziz Center for Knowledge and Culture (Ithra), Dhahran, Saudi Arabia, 2009

The King Abdulaziz Center for Knowledge and Culture (Ithra)[1] is currently the most advanced of Snøhetta's projects in the Middle East region, and captures the thoughts discussed in this article both as a process and as form. It reinvents traditional elements such as courtyards and smaller oasis gardens, and uses traditional construction methods such as rammed earth, while at the same time introducing new elements relevant to its functions, but always in relationship to the recognisable metaphors of their totality. The project clearly shows how the existing desert landscape is a plane of reference for both the building and programme. The elliptical monoscape surrounding the complex is derived from the desert, but unlike the desert it is not a cultural zero-point, but saturated with content.

The centre is developed around a series of pebble-like shapes, structurally and metaphorically supporting each other, similar to the stones of a Roman arch. The smallest pebble is the keystone, a space for debating challenges related to young leadership, and, if it was removed, the whole complex would collapse. Each pebble further contains a separate function: library, temporary exhibition, concert and performing arts hall and the lifelong learning tower. All lean on each other, transforming vertical forces into horizontal ones before finally carrying them into the foundations.

This paralleled transition of forces and functions maintains both the individuality of each pebble as well as their collectiveness. They are singulars supporting the plural.

To emphasise this feature, each volume is clad with the same material within the same system yet with distinctive individual results. Semi-shiny stainless-steel pipes, 67 millimetres (2.6 inches) in diameter, wrap each pebble in a continuous manner. The geometry of each pattern is defined by three parameters: the geometrical shape of the pebble; the shape of the entrance opening into the pebble; and the starting point of the line wrapping along the shape of this opening. Each pebble gets its own fingerprint pattern distinguishing it clearly from its neighbour. This cladding provides both shade and ventilation for the insulated walls behind, but it also collects solar heat, reaching surface temperatures around 80°C (176°F). The surface heat becomes part of the visual experience of the building, mirroring the heat waves and creating air mirages shivering like an aura around the pebbles. Further development will show if this heat may also be extracted efficiently from the facades to provide energy to the building and to cool the interior. Whenever there is a window opening, the pipes are conically flattened to generate brise-soleils in front of the glass. For maintenance of the facades, Snøhetta is currently developing facade robots to continuously move along the pipes while cleaning them.

The second important element of the complex, the entrance, is sunken partially into the ground. All entrances into the different functions are directly connected to this public space which is clad entirely with rammed earth providing stable temperature and humidity. The stainless-steel pebbles penetrating the plaza are in strong contrast to the rammed earth, thus capturing both archaic and high-tech expressions within the same space.

Throughout the design process, contradictions within the project have triggered discussions of content, technologies and functional relationships rather than form. The expression of the building complex has seldom been questioned and it has been as if its physical presence has embedded itself as an innate part of a possible future environment. ⚙

Note
1. Under the auspices of the client, oil company Saudi Aramco, which has also had members of its project management team located within the offices of Snøhetta in Oslo, it has been possible to develop Snøhetta's competition scheme into a fully designed project, currently under construction.

The keystone is the key element in the geometry of the
pebble composition. It is the only pebble that is lifted
above the monosurface, giving great importance to its
content, and is programmatically linked to the library
as a dialogue, discussion and contemplation space.

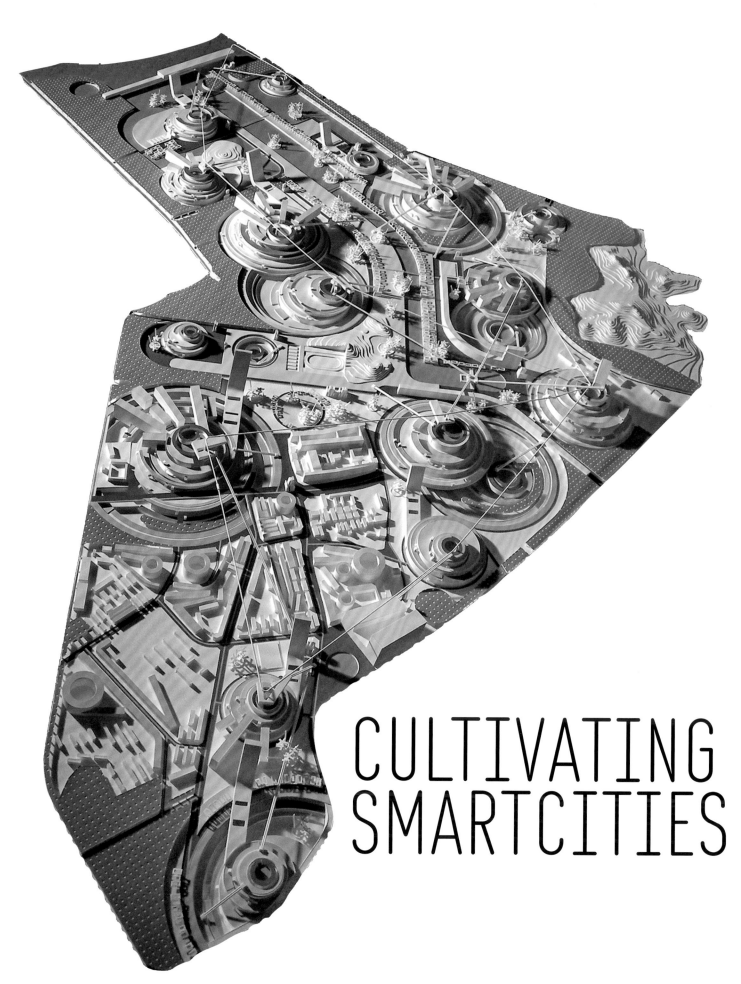

CULTIVATING
SMARTCITIES

CJ Lim

CJ Lim/Studio 8 Architects, Guangming
Smartcity, Shenzhen, China, 2007
A new urban typology commissioned by
the Shenzhen Municipal Planning Bureau,
covering 8 square kilometres (3 square miles)
of Shenzhen to house 200,000 inhabitants
combining agricultural tradition and 21st-
century living. Farming suburbs in the form of
self-sufficient towers and craters augment the
natural landscape to exploit the climatic context,
and are linked by sky buses and funiculars.

On 9 April 2009, Michelle Obama planted the first
seedlings of onion, lettuce, peas and peppers in the
102-square-metre (1,100-square-foot) White House
Kitchen Garden. She may have planted the green
shoots for a smartcity. **CJ Lim**, author of *Smartcities +
Eco-warriors* (Routledge, 2010), describes sustainable
urban developments in the form of smartcities – a new
urban exuberance reintegrating cultivated land within
an urban economic and ecological context system.
These verdant edible edifices of urban spatial theatre
are aesthetically and culturally engaging. Soliciting an
emotional as well as intellectual response they have the
potential to connect with the public and involve them
in the architectural possibilities of the city.

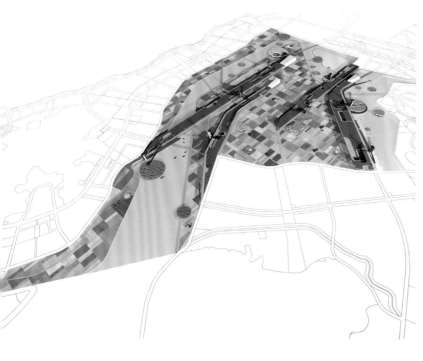

CJ Lim/Studio 8 Architects, Central
Open Space, Multifunctional Administrative
City (MAC), Republic of Korea, 2007
Proposal for the 7-square-kilometre (2.7-square-
mile) public green core of the MAC funded by
the Government Administrative City Agency and
Korean Land Corporation. The aim is to create an
'arable kitchen-garden park' while also preserving
the area's historic and cultural identity.

Floating Mob
Town Hall + M

Suburb Squar
Municipal Fac

Commercial -
30 to 100m w
Office Space

Housing Block
average of 50
and 5 Villas (

Nursery

Nursery Playi

Flower Garde

Swimming Po

Playground o

Flower Beds e

Sky-Bus Stopi

Sports Fields

Arable Kitche

Lawn Ribbon-
System (Bioga

Fruit Orchard

Beach

Board Walk - e
culminating in
Access. Buggi

Road - leading

Urban Plaza -
a flexible, ped
Housing Block

0m   125

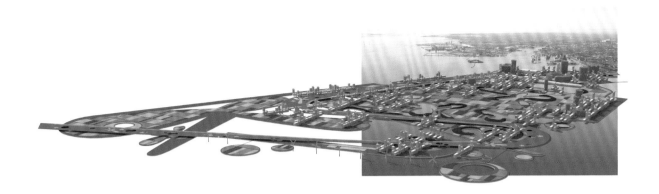

At time of writing, more than half of mankind, some 3.3 billion people, are living in urban areas. By 2030, this is expected to swell to almost 5 billion.[1] We are simultaneously experiencing a global food crisis resulting from low productivity, government policies diverting food crops to the creation of biofuels, climate change and growing food demand brought on by an exponentially expanding population. The world is heading for a drop in agricultural production of 20 to 40 per cent, depending on the severity and length of the current global droughts. Developed nations have abandoned all notion of self-sufficiency and are hugely dependent on imported food, while food-producing nations are imposing food export restrictions. Food prices will soar and, in poor countries with food deficits, millions will starve.[2]

The hybridisation of agriculture and the establishment of the city-dwelling farmer can lead to an association that is symbiotic rather than parasitic, reducing carbon emissions and food shortage in addition to providing less tangible yet equally significant environmental and social benefits. Urban agriculture will result in food immediacy within cities, providing nutrition and health benefits. It will create job opportunities, generate income for urban poverty groups and provide a social safety net. The communal creation and maintenance of a productive landscape offers a means to cultivate a larger responsibility among each and every one of us, repairing a diverse and fractured society. Planning and design of smartcities are delivered by all, no longer the exclusive remit of the planner or designer. Neighbourhood food programmes, community allotments and farmers' markets foster community spirit; social inclusion of disadvantaged groups and community development will be facilitated. The result is a new sustainable urban exuberance.

In an economically sensitive climate, design needs to offer intelligent solutions that focus on need and demonstrate added environmentally sustainable value to regain public and political confidence. Cities are calling out for a new formal, textural and experiential exuberance with nature. At its most simplistic level, the design positions farming within the city, taking advantage of beneficial adjacencies between programme and function. Urban solid waste and greywater can be used as fertiliser and irrigation; food transport and associated carbon emissions are removed from the equation.

Adam and Eve did not have to go far for sustenance, for everything was aplenty in the Garden of Eden, where every type of tree, pleasing to the eye and good for food, was planted. The desire for fresh healthy food has been in existence since time immemorial. Refrigeration and rapid transport systems have, to a certain extent, made time and distance an irrelevance. However, processing, packaging, transportation and storage account for 80 per cent of the energy used to place food on the kitchen table. Produce travels an average of 2,092 to 3,219 kilometres (1,300 to 2,000 miles) from farmer to consumer. A new breed of individual, the citizen farmer, harvesting crops from the concrete jungle, will cut unnecessary carbon emissions in a single stroke, while providing ready access to nutritional, seasonal and flavoursome produce. There will be no second, third and fourth parties responsible for the commoditisation, giving a new meaning to hand-to-mouth existence. As city dwellers, we need to re-engage with the exuberance of fresh local produce and the roots of our sustenance in a way that does not involve abstract bite-size ready meals.

Conventional agriculture is hugely dependent on water resources, and water

CJ Lim/Studio 8 Architects, Nordhavnen Smartcity, Copenhagen, Denmark, 2008
A 1.7-square-kilometre (0.6-square-mile) 'arable kitchen-garden park' for the Copenhagen Port Authority espousing sustainable farming principles on a former industrial and ship-docking yard. More than 80 per cent of the ground is dedicated to vegetable farming, interspersed with grazing fields. Compact car-free suburb clusters are stitched together by an elevated ribbon of lawn draped with hydroponic curtains.

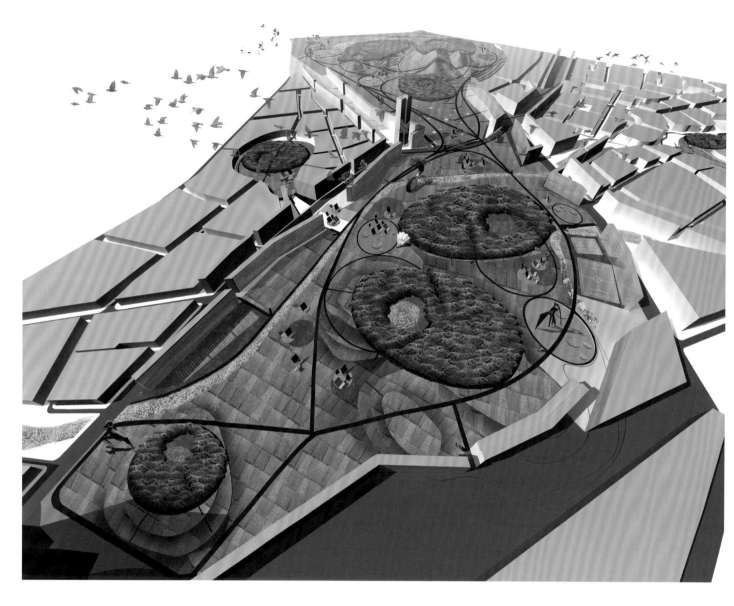

CJ Lim/Studio 8 Architects,
Guangming Sustainable Arable
Park, Shenzhen, China, 2008
The rejuvenation of existing but
underused green space with ripples
of environmental and landscape
strategies that spread out into
the city. The park is reconfigured
into landscaped clusters with new
flexible programmes such as organic
gardening, energy production and
public landscape art.

For the smartcities programme to be identifiable and to successfully foster societal cohesion, the public realm must be fully reclaimed. Tired existing cities can be re-energised and new sustainable developments can flourish through exuberant productive urban greening and the cultivation of green open spaces.

management is identified by a UN world development report as mankind's most serious challenge of the 21st century;[3] the impermeability of the urban fabric – roads, roofs, hard standing and the concrete landscape – constitutes flood risks due to the inability of these elements to attenuate surface water. Again, the design solution is startlingly apparent. Vegetation, edible or otherwise, is a ready-made natural sustainable drainage system, harvesting rainfall and mediating extreme temperatures as well as being the most efficient photovoltaic cell currently available to us by virtue of chlorophyll's photosynthetic properties – a demonstration of exuberance in nature.

Urban agriculture is not a new phenomenon; its popularity and adoption has waxed and waned over the millennia, from the recycling of urban wastes and tunnel irrigation networks in ancient Persia for agriculture, to the stepped cities and farming terraces of Machu Picchu that can be considered as a precursor to hydroponics. Proposed intervention sites vary considerably in scale and context. Within dense urban areas, roof tops, windowsills, balconies and walls can be appropriated for the growth of edible crops, evoking the spirit of the Second World War victory garden when America was still in the midst of the Great Depression. In a remarkably ambitious programme, gardening classes, literature, seeds, fertiliser and committees were organised, yielding 40 per cent of the country's non-military produce at the time.

For the smartcities programme to be identifiable and to successfully foster societal cohesion, the public realm must be fully reclaimed. Tired existing cities can be re-energised and new sustainable developments can flourish through exuberant productive urban greening and the cultivation of green open spaces. Plazas, parks, waterfronts, boats, car parks and greyfield sites where appropriate sunlight levels are available are all viable locations for cultivation. The metrics of urban exuberance will be clearly manifest, growing before our eyes while beautifying our environment, providing nutrition and facilitating social interaction.

In peri-urban areas, the intervention is more profound and far-reaching. New housing developments can be planned to integrate farming at the scale of landscape. Buildings can be planted into the natural topography, surfaced in growing media, oriented to receive or protect from sunlight, and integrating water conservation and waste recycling components. In addition to supplying food for consumption and commodity, energy demand can be dramatically reduced. With food production concentrated in urban and peri-urban areas, agricultural land in outlying areas can be used for the growth of biofuels, without causing deforestation abroad.

Keeping a nation at the vanguard of food production, and creating a model that can be replicated worldwide, requires the transference of food production towards our cities, saving consumers and manufacturers tens of billions of dollars per year and keeping wastage to a minimum. The exuberance of the intervention is to promote the environmental and social, rather than the purely financial. The solution of sustainable and environmentally responsible growth lies within the multilayered programmatic exuberance of smartcities – the embedding of mutually supporting closed systems within our urban environment. We all want to live in this new exuberant smartcity, so let's start cultivating. ∆

Notes
1. UNFPA, *State of World Population: Peering into the Dawn of an Urban Millennium*, 2007.
2. See http://www.globalresearch.ca/index. php?context=va&aid=12252.
3. *The United Nations World Water Development Report: Water for People, Water for Life*, 2003.

Judith Clark is a reader in the field of fashion and museology at the London College of Fashion. She is an associate lecturer at IUAV in Venice and teaches within the History and Theory Department at the Architectural Association. She is the founder of the Judith Clark Costume Gallery, where she has curated 20 exhibitions between 1997 and 2002. Other exhibitions she has curated include 'Spectres: When Fashion Turns Back' (V&A and Momu Antwerp), 'Anna Piaggi Fashion-ology' (V&A), 'Simonetta: La Prima Donna della moda Italiana' (Palazzo Pitti, Florence) and 'Installing Allusions (Boijmans van Beuningen Museum, Rotterdam).

Sir Peter Cook is a founder member of Archigram. His architectural studies at Bournemouth College of Art were followed by those at the Architectural Association in London where he subsequently taught from 1964 to 1990. From 1984 to 2004 he was Professor of Architecture at the Staedelschule in Frankfurt, and from 1990 to 2006 Bartlett Professor and Chair of the Bartlett School of Architecture, UCL. As member of Archigram he was awarded the RIBA Royal Gold Medal. He has also received the Jean Tschumi Medal of the UIA and the RIBA Annie Spink award. He is a Commandeur d'ordre des arts et letters of France, and was made a Knight Bachelor in the Queen's Birthday Honours in 2007. He has published innumerable books and his work has been exhibited worldwide.

Hernan Diaz Alonso is the principal and founder of the Xefirotarch practice based in Los Angeles. He is a Distinguished Professor of Architecture and the Graduate Thesis coordinator at SCI-Arc, Los Angeles, Design Studio Professor at the GSAPP at Columbia University, and Studio Professor at the University of Applied Arts, Vienna. His architectural designs have received numerous awards and have been exhibited in both architecture and art museums. His work has also been widely published, including in the monograph *Xefirotarch:Excessive* (Huazhong University of Science and Technology Press, 2008), and featured in many solo exhibitions internationally, as well as in numerous permanent collections. In 2005 Diaz Alonso was the winner of the PS1 MoMA Young Architects Program.

Robert Greenwood is a partner and Senior Design Director at Snøhetta. He was involved with the Alexandria Library project and also directed the Sandvika Cultural House and Hamar Town Hall. He is now Project Leader for the firm's Ras Al Khaimah Gateway project and the King Abdulaziz Center for Knowledge and Culture.

Robert Harbison is Professor of Architectural History at London Metropolitan University and the author of many books including *The Built, the Unbuilt and the Unbuildable* (MIT Press, 1991), *Eccentric Spaces* (MIT Press, 2000), *Reflections on Baroque* (Reaktion, 2002) and *Travels in the History of Architecture* (Reaktion, 2009).

CJ Lim is Professor of Architecture and Cultural Design at the Bartlett School of Architecture, UCL, and the founder of Studio 8 Architects, a multidisciplinary practice in urban planning, architecture and landscape focusing on interpretations of cultural, social and environmental sustainability. He is internationally acclaimed for the designs of his smartcities, and his recent award-winning eco-urban planning for the Chinese and Korean governments. He is the author of eight books, the most recent of which is *Smartcities and Eco-warriors* (Routledge, 2010).

Wolf D Prix is a co-founder of Coop Himmelb(l)au. He studied architecture at the Vienna University of Technology, the Architectural Association of London and the Southern California Institute of Architecture (SCI-Arc) in Los Angeles. After teaching abroad he became Professor of the University of Applied Arts, Vienna, in 1993, where he now serves as Vice-Rector and Head of the Institute for Architecture. He has received numerous awards and his work with Coop Himmelb(l)au has been featured in many museums and collections worldwide. His work has also been published in many books including *Get Off My Cloud* (Hatje Cantz, 2005) and *Dynamic Forces: BMW Welt (Prestel, 2007).*

Ali Rahim is an architect, a director of Contemporary Architecture Practice and a member of the permanent architecture design faculty at the University of Pennsylvania where he directs design research studios and coordinates the final year of the Master of Architecture Design Program. He has served as the Studio Hadid Visiting Professor at the University of Applied Arts, Vienna, as Louis I Kahn Visiting Architecture Professor at Yale University and Visiting Architecture Professor at Harvard University. His books include *Catalytic Formations: Architecture and Digital Design* (Taylor & Francis, 2006) and *AD Elegance* (2007), co-edited with Hina Jamelle, *AD Contemporary Techniques in Architecture* (2002) and *AD Contemporary Processes in Architecture* (2000).

Yael Reisner has a PhD in architecture from RMIT, Melbourne, a Diploma and RIBA Part 2 from the Architectural Association in London, and a BSc in biology from Hebrew University in Jerusalem. Practising in London, she currently teaches internationally after nine years of teaching architectural design at the Bartlett School of Architecture, UCL (MArch and Studio Master of Diploma Unit 11). Her book, *Architecture and Beauty: Conversations with Architects About a Troubled Relationship*, written with Fleur Watson, is to be published by John Wiley & Sons Ltd in 2010.

Neil Spiller is Professor of Architecture and Digital Theory and a practising architect. He is the Graduate Director of Design, Director of the Advanced Virtual and Technological Architecture Research Group (AVATAR) and Vice Dean at the Bartlett School of Architecture, UCL. His books include *Visionary Architecture: Blueprints of the Modern Imagination* (Thames & Hudson, 2006) and *Digital Architecture NOW* (Thames & Hudson, 2008), a compendium of contemporary digital architectural practice.

Kjetil Trædal Thorsen is a founding partner of Snøhetta and has directed such high-profile projects as the Alexandria Library and the Norwegian National Opera in Oslo. He has been instrumental in defining and developing Snøhetta's philosophy and architectural ambition. From 2004 to 2008 he was also professor at the Institute for Experimental Architecture at the University of Innsbruck .

Tom Wiscombe is an architectural designer based in Los Angeles. In 1999 he founded EMERGENT, a platform for exploring contemporary models of biology, engineering and computation to produce an architecture characterised by formal variability, integration of building systems and atmospheric effects. EMERGENT has developed an international profile via a widely recognised *oeuvre* of competition entries and installations, including the MoMA/PS1 Urban Beach in 2003. The office's work is part of the permanent collection of MoMA, New York. Wiscombe was Chief Designer at Coop Himmelb(l)au for more than 10 years, where he was in charge of design for BMW World. He currently teaches at SCI-Arc in Los Angeles.

LEADING LADY
MONICA PIDGEON, EDITOR OF ARCHITECTURAL DESIGN, 1946 TO 1975

Monica Pidgeon in the *AD* offices around 1960. The magazine was produced in the same single room in Bloomsbury from the early 1930s right through to the mid-1970s.

Peter Murray pays tribute to Monica Pidgeon (1913–2009). Editor of *Architectural Design* for almost three decades, Monica was responsible for establishing *Architectural Design* as the premier international architectural magazine. Murray highlights her immense contribution to architecture over the years, as well as evoking the experience of working for Monica as one of her 'boys', or technical editors.

For most of its existence, *AD* has been a magazine about ideas. That, I believe, is Monica Pidgeon's great legacy. Through its pages she promulgated the ideas of the MARS (Modern Architectural Research) group, CIAM (Congrès International de l'Architecture Moderne), Team 10, Buckminster Fuller, John Turner, Cedric Price, Archigram, Christopher Alexander, Carl Popper, the Japanese Metabolists, and ideas about climate change and sustainability long before they became common currency. The architecture that she published emerged out of the big ideas that she and her technical editors espoused.

I arrived at *Architectural Design* in 1969 to take up a job as assistant art editor. The editorial office was one large room in an Edwardian block off Bloomsbury Way, close to the British Museum and 10 minutes' walk from the Architectural Association in Bedford Square. The area was pretty run-down at the time as it was due for demolition under plans by Colin St John Wilson – later dropped in

Le Corbusier addressing the 8th CIAM conference at Hoddesdon, Hertfordshire, in 1951. Monica helped to organise the event and is seated in the front row.

Monica with Ken Frampton (left) judging the *AD* Project Awards in 1964. The Project Awards were an important springboard for young architects in the 1960s.

Nikolaus Pevsner, Buckminster Fuller (in a distinctive pose) and Louis Kahn at a meeting of the Jerusalem Committee.

Monica with Bill Howell. Howell was a member of Team 10 and a partner in the practice of Howell, Killick Partidge and Amis.

favour of relocation to St Pancras – to build the proposed British Library as an extension to the museum complex. The editorial team worked around a large table at one end of the room; the art department at a long worktop under the windows overlooking the street. We worked very civilised hours – starting at 11am and finishing at 7pm.

My recollection of Monica at that time is of her sitting at the table, scissors and galley proofs in hand, Sellotape dispenser in front of her, preparing draft layouts for the art department. While she was working, her spectacles were perched at the end of her nose and as people walked into the room she would look over the top of her glasses, peering at them in a schoolmarmish sort of way. She could be a bit like a headmistress, and she was tough. She disliked feebleness, and secretaries were frequently in tears following a stern telling off. She was also fearless. I

remember one day when Ernö Goldfinger – a man so fearsome that Ian Fleming named his Bond villain after him – stormed into the office deeply unhappy about the treatment we had given one of his buildings. Monica robustly defended our position, never letting on that I was the person responsible for Goldfinger's ire.

It seems that almost every day some major figure from the world of architecture would drop by the office to say hello to Monica and show her their latest projects.

Visitors would be invited to sit on the chair next to Monica, the first version of Arne Jacobsen's Ant chair, which only had three legs. There was regular amusement in the office when a leading figure of the day, leaning forward to explain a detail on his drawings, would awkwardly slide under the editorial table as the, now illegal, tripod gave way.

Monica took over the magazine in 1946 and subsequently built up a huge network of architects and correspondents. She was very active on the architectural scene. She was one of the organisers of the founding meeting of the Union International des Architectes (UIA) in Lausanne in 1948; she attended all the CIAM meetings and was an active member of the MARS group. Although she supported Team X, she refused to attend their meetings since she disapproved of their attacks on CIAM. She met Bucky Fuller in 1961 and regularly published his work thereafter.

Monica was an internationalist. She was born in Chile of a French father, Andre Lehman, the manager of a copper mine, and a Scottish mother. In 1929 the family moved to England for Monica to properly complete her education. She went to the Bartlett School of Architecture where Albert Richardson was professor. Richardson placed her in the interior design department which he thought more suitable than architecture for a woman. Her contemporaries were Hugh Casson, Richard Seifert and a handsome student called Raymond Pidgeon whom she married in 1936.

In Hollywood with engineer Konrad Wachsmann when she went to record him for the Pidgeon Audio Visual series of engineers' talks. The results of the meeting can still be heard on www.pidgeondigital.com.

Monica with the two major women architects of the postwar period: Alison Smithson (left) and Jane Drew (right). All were attending a conference of women architects in Iran.

Monica worked as a furniture designer up to the outbreak of war, when she went to *AD* as assistant to the editor, Tony Towndrow. During that time she had two children: Carl, who was to become an eminent physicist, and Annabel, who was to marry the architectural photographer John Donat. She divorced Pidgeon in 1946. She was promoted to editor in 1946 when Towndrow emigrated to Australia, but it was with the appointment of Theo Crosby as technical editor in 1953 that the organisation of the magazine took on the form that was to shape its editorial policies for the next 20 years.

Crosby was a significant figure on the architectural and art scenes in the 1950s. He curated, with Reyner Banham, the highly influential 'This is Tomorrow' exhibition at the Whitechapel Gallery (August 1956), bringing together the work of artists and architects including Goldfinger, James Stirling, Eduardo Paolozzi, Richard Hamilton, Colin St John Wilson and the Smithsons.

Monica with Teddy Kollek, the mayor of Jerusalem, in the early 1970s. She was a member of the committee set up by Kollek to advise on the planning of the Israeli capital.

In 1961, the UIA congress was held on the South Bank in London and Monica was closely involved in organising and hosting the event. It was there that she met Buckminster Fuller. Fuller was in town to launch his World Design Science Decade which proposed that architectural schools around the world be encouraged to carry out a 10-year study into how the world's resources could be distributed more fairly. It was just the sort of grand idea that suited *AD*'s international view.

Monica revisited South America in 1962. In Peru she met the housing architect John Turner who showed her the self-build shantytowns of Lima – the *barriadas*. Turner was studying how these informal building techniques could be harnessed to provide better-quality housing as well as humane urban planning. This was to be another theme that threaded through *AD*'s issues over the next decade. Her connections with Chile were renewed later in the decade when she advised President Allende on the choice of architects who could help resolve the country's housing crisis. The result was a study by the architect and writer Martin Pawley who proposed commandeering the car industry to manufacture prefabricated homes. But Allende's death in the coup of 1973 brought the project to an abrupt end. From 1971 to 1976 Monica was a member of a group of international experts, including Buckminster Fuller, Nikolaus Pevsner, Louis Kahn and Moshe Safdie, brought together by Mayor Teddy Kollek to advise on the replanning of Jerusalem.

Monica gave great freedom to her technical editors, her 'boys' – Crosby, Ken Frampton, Robin Middleton, myself and Martin Spring, to follow our particular enthusiasms within the magazine. Ken Frampton took over in 1962 and moved *AD*'s content away from Crosby's slant on art and architecture to a focus on the buildings

David Dean (RIBA librarian), Monica, Leonard Manasseh and John Partridge at the RIBA during the time that she was editor of the institute's journal.

themselves. Robin Middleton succeeded Frampton in 1964.

During the late 1960s and early 1970s the magazine had a close and symbiotic relationship with the Architectural Association as Alvin Boyarsky set about creating the educational establishment that was to have such a significant impact on the architecture of the latter part of the century. The economic and oil crises of that period decimated *AD*'s advertising revenue and the owners, the Standard Catalogue Company, threatened to close the magazine. Monica convinced them to keep it running on a 'book' economy. This meant covering all costs from copy sales and giving up on advertising revenue, and is the way the magazine operates to this day.

However, survival was tough and by 1975 Monica had had enough. She accepted an invitation from Eric Lyons to edit the *RIBA Journal* and stayed there until 1979 when I succeeded her.

When she 'retired', Monica made use of her amazing list of contacts. She had often thought that the inspirational talks of architects should be enjoyed by a wider audience. So she started Pidgeon Audio Visual (PAV) which published packs of slides and tapes in which architects and designers talked about their work. The packs were distributed to schools of architecture around the world. She continued to add to the recordings until she was in her late eighties. The full catalogue includes contributions by Reyner Banham, Walter Bor, Alan Fletcher, Maxwell Fry and Buckminster Fuller. Monica asked me to take over the project and in 2006 work started on the digitisation of the Pidgeon archive which, now almost complete, can be accessed on www.pidgeondigital.com. The complete archive is not only a testament to Monica's wide-ranging enthusiasm for architects and

Monica at an Architectural Association (AA) exhibition opening in the early 1970s. Alvin Boyarsky, then chairman of the AA, can be seen in the background.

architecture, it brings to life a whole generation of architects and their thinking in a way that the printed media cannot.

Although the great enthusiasms and world-changing strategies of the international movement, of which Monica Pidgeon was a close witness, foundered, she never lost her view that architecture and architects were agents of social change and improvement rather than mere decorators and formgivers.

Monica was made an Honorary Fellow of the RIBA in 1970, of the Architectural Association in 1979, and of the AIA, for her work on Pidgeon Audio Visual, in 1987. Δ+

Monica Pidgeon, architectural editor, born 29 September 1913; died 17 September 2009.

Peter Murray worked at *AD* from 1969 to 1974. He was editor of the *RIBA Journal* from 1979 to 1983, and founder publisher of *Blueprint* magazine, 1983–90. He is currently chairman of design and communications consultancy Wordsearch, and of New London Architecture. He is founder director of the London Festival of Architecture and editor of Pidgeon Digital.

MORPHOSIS ARCHITECTS' COOPER UNION ACADEMIC BUILDING, NEW YORK

Thom Mayne and his colleagues have packed a lot of architecture and a number of very practical spaces into one small city block in the firm's first major New York building. **Jayne Merkel** describes the dramatic skylighted central staircase that sweeps through the new academic building for the prestigious Cooper Union for the Advancement of Science and Art, surrounded by efficient classroom, office and studio space with exciting views of the city all around.

Jayne Merkel

From the street, the new Cooper Union academic building, which houses the Albert Nerken School of Engineering and the Faculty of Humanities and Social Sciences, looks jagged and angular and rather dark, since it is sheathed in a perforated, patterned stainless-steel skin that folds in and out over glass-walled interior spaces and cuts away with several large gashes. Inside, however, the building is flooded with light from a triangular glass roof over a gigantic twisting central staircase. It is as if an inverted tornado had blown through the structure, tearing apart a neat concrete staircase so that the steps were bent and the roof of the building was blown away. Although there are elevators that make express stops and ones that open on every floor, the skylighted central staircase is meant to be the main physical and social connector of the building which houses art studios and laboratories, flexible classrooms and faculty offices, art galleries, meeting rooms and an auditorium, and also has several outdoor roof-top spaces.

Some look out on the original 1859 brownstone Greek Revival Cooper Union Building (30 Cooper Square) across the street, where the famous art, architecture and engineering school was founded. Its stacks of arcades in various sizes containing architecture studios, offices and classrooms topped by a sawtooth roof make it a particularly light and airy structure for its time. But with the exception of its famous multicolumned underground auditorium where Abraham Lincoln once spoke, the entire interior is modern – white walled, crisply geometric and spatially complex. It was rebuilt by the late Cooper Union architecture school dean, John Hejduk, in 1975 and, like the school it houses, is one of New York City's gems.

A spiralling atrium sweeps through the new building filling the entire interior with light and physically connecting the activities on all nine levels with a central staircase and 'skybridges'. But in the spirit of the mystery suggested by the facade, the atrium is just out of view of the entrance. Its south wall is covered with perforated glass-fibre-reinforced gypsum acoustical panelling on the inside and glass-fibre-reinforced concrete panelling on the outside of the building.

The angular central staircase, which sweeps from the ground level through the third floor, is enveloped in and defined by a porous 'mega mesh' lattice wall, ingeniously composed of a combination of straight and curved steel tubes. Contractors devised a clever system to build it, sliding steel balls precisely on to the horizontal pipes, welding them in place, and connecting the diagonals with the steel balls, then covering them all with glass-fibre-reinforced gypsum to create the diamond profile of the moulded form.

So Thom Mayne and his colleagues at the Santa Monica, California-based firm Morphosis had a hard act to follow in a part of Greenwich Village laden with history and ambitious recent buildings by Herzog & de Meuron, SANAA, Carlos Zapata, Gwathmey Siegel and others. The boxy yellow-brick structure nearby that used to house the Cooper engineering school is to be replaced by a 13-storey polygonal commercial office building by Fumihiko Maki.

Mayne's decision to compete by creating the most dramatic structure in the neighbourhood (and one that does not take its cues from its surroundings in an obvious way) is the least well-conceived aspect of the project. Since there is plenty of action inside, some even visible from the outside, it would have been more subtle – and even more exciting – to do something with character that becomes apparent gradually. But subtlety has never been Morphosis' calling card. Also, it is not as if this site needs a quiet presence since the part of Third Avenue that separates the two Cooper Union buildings is wide enough for the new one not to overpower the old. And 41 Cooper Square, as the new building is called, complements its predecessor in terms of facilities, if not aesthetics.

Since the old building does not have a big informal central gathering space, Mayne has provided a dazzling one that also ties together the myriad facilities and school communities, filling the building with natural light, air and energy. Its intriguingly contorted form is supported by steel framing and surrounded by a gargantuan white spider's web, called the atrium 'mega mesh', an ingenious combination of straight and curved tubes that define it while leaving it open to the classrooms and offices along the outer walls.

Above the third floor, the staircase narrows to form 'skybridges', narrow concrete staircases that link the various levels and facilities. These are framed by backlighted Plexiglas panels under the railings, instead of the thin steel webs that frame balconies on the lower floors. Balcony railings here are also sheathed in backlighted Plexiglas panels, so that the walkways glow, further energising the upper storeys.

Most of the other interior spaces are very practical, rectangular and rather low-ceilinged in order to fit the ambitious programme into a 54.8-metre (180-foot) long, 30.5-metre (100-foot) deep and 36.5-metre (120-foot) tall envelope allowed by zoning on this unusually tiny block. There is a small 200-seat auditorium with a crinkled metal mesh ceiling and walls, which is underground like the larger historic one across the street. There is also a large divisible subterranean art gallery that is fetchingly visible both from inside the entrance and from the outside on Seventh Street, where a row of quaint little 19th-century storefronts includes McSorley's, the oldest pub in the city. Two floors below ground are laboratories and workshops.

Much of the ground floor is devoted to the entry area, where a big rounded reception desk leads to the welcoming 6-metre (20-foot) wide staircase. Four adaptable classrooms line the back (east) wall. A narrow staircase leading to the underground areas is tucked in on the west side, where there is also a double-height retail space opening on to Third Avenue. That takes up much of the first floor, too, though there are also classrooms, deans' and faculty offices there. More deans' and faculty offices surround the next level where there are additional classrooms. Upstairs, in the 16,258-square-metre (175,000-square-foot) building, which has eight storeys above the ground level, there are more classrooms, unusually energy-efficient laboratories, offices, lounges and a computer centre which students from all disciplines share. The art studios are at the top where there is also a

The staircase off the entrance overlooks the old Cooper Union Building across Third Avenue (in the background). On the upper storeys, the staircase narrows to become a series of narrow footbridges linking the sides of the buildings as well as the various levels. Large tubular railings relate to the scale of the city, small ones fit comfortably into students' hands.

At dusk, 41 Cooper Square looks brighter and more welcoming than it does during the day. The convoluted, perforated stainless-steel skin, which projects as much as 2.4 metres (8 feet) in some areas and less than half a metre in others (especially on the north, south and east sides), reveals the activity inside and the regular column grid behind the window wall that takes over from the V-shaped columns at the bottom of the second floor, which rest on transfer beams below. Floor framing consists of a cast-in-place reinforced-concrete one-way slab system supported by beams and flat two-way reinforced concrete slabs.

The entry area is very visible from Third Avenue under the perforated stainless-steel skin overlaid with an irregular pattern of rectangular patches that are more opaque because they have smaller perforations. These patches are intended to relate to small windows in nearby buildings. Above the ground floor, part of the name of the building folds under the vertical surface, which appears to be supported by the slanted concrete columns that actually hold up the structural grid inside.

living green roof terrace with a gigantic stone eagle recovered from New York's beloved but long since demolished Pennsylvania Railroad Station.

In all these spaces the main event is the view beyond, which is usually easy to see despite the energy-saving perforated stainless-steel skin in front of the double-paned glass walls. From the inside, the building is much more light-filled than it appears from the outside, even in places where the skin is not cut away.

The concrete frame, though invisible in most places, is supported by very visible, daring-looking V-shaped exterior columns that extend inside to the bottom of the second floor where a rectangular structural grid takes over. When the building opened, these sloping supports provided a tempting challenge to skateboarders whose constant, if unsuccessful, attempts to scale them created a dreadful din and fast-moving traffic on the extra-wide sidewalk that was intended to provide another informal gathering space. Recently, the Cooper staff and local police have been deterring the would-be urban athletes, but the design does pose a problem.

The edgy sport somehow fits the spirit of the edgy facade, but it is unlikely to be compatible with the very rigorous intellectual activity that takes place inside the building's flexible, state-of-the-art laboratories, studios and classrooms made of renewable, recycled, low-emission materials. Radiant heating and cooling panels on the ceilings introduce new efficient HVAC technology to the US. A cogeneration plant provides power, recovers wasted heat and saves energy. A green roof insulates, while reducing 'heat island' effect, stormwater runoff and pollutants, and its water is reused. Together these measures make the building 40 per cent more energy efficient than most buildings of this type.

Even the aesthetic effects contribute. The dramatic skylighted central staircase improves the flow of air and daylighting while providing vertical circulation and a place to exchange glances, greetings and ideas. The perforated skin closes automatically to reduce heat radiation in summer and admit more sunlight in winter. The panels, which open up to 90 degrees, are controlled by the building management system (BMS) on a timetable established by a detailed sun study for every hour of the day throughout the year. School officials can override the controls manually in a snowstorm or other event when they want to keep all panels closed or open.

Although 41 Cooper Square will be the first LEED-certified academic building in New York City (and may achieve the highest Platinum rating), Morphosis does not design specifically to LEED guidelines the way many commercial practices do. The firm's approach is more unique and more technologically advanced in many ways, and yet it has managed to create an unusually energy-efficient, extremely practical and very exciting building on a modest budget, reputed to be $150 million – a real bargain in New York. ⚠+

WINTER OLYMPIC BUILDINGS, VANCOUVER 2010

Visiting Vancouver in advance of the 2010 Winter Olympics, **David Littlefield** discovered that the city was pressing two architectural agendas particularly hard: legacy and timber – the Canadian Northwest's principal natural resource.

David Littlefield

Canon Design, Richmond Olympic Oval, Richmond, British Columbia, 2008
The roof of this 33,000-square-metre (355,220-square-foot) building, the 2010 speed-skating area, is constructed largely of timber; each of the glulam beams is assembled from four elements.

'Right now, you're looking at something that's only half built.' Darryl Condon, architect of Vancouver's new curling centre, was speaking in August 2009 of a building that would serve as a major Winter Olympics venue in February 2010. Only half built? That, in fact, was the intention. Condon, principal at Hughes Condon Marler Architects, took the view that the Olympics is a travelling theatre – a televised spectacle framed within camera angles, banners, flags and temporary seating. He felt no need to actually finish a building that would barely be visible beneath the costume of the Games. But Condon was doing more than giving himself time – he was scheduling the building so that it would provide one particular set of spaces during construction, and a very different spatial arrangement upon completion. This capacious Olympic shed will, when the Games have departed, be subdivided and fitted out as a community centre offering a wide range of sports facilities as well as a preschool unit and public library.

This careful phasing was part of British Columbia's legacy strategy for the Games. This year's Olympic skating, hockey and curling events were located in the city of Vancouver itself, a couple of hours' drive from the outdoor skiing events taking place in and around Whistler. Canadian officials, like their UK counterparts planning for 2012, were determined not to build any white elephants or super-equipped facilities far from anywhere. It is difficult for people in the UK to appreciate the importance of skating (and curling, incidentally) to Canadian national life; these sports are enormously popular and incredibly competitive. Consequently, most communities have their own rinks, many of which are now ageing and in need of repair or replacement. Hosting the Winter Olympics therefore provided Vancouver with the impetus to update key community facilities, locating world-class venues within relatively quiet suburbs, or at least within easy reach.

Condon's Olympic building, located in Vancouver's Hillcrest Park, is arguably the cleverest response to this emphasis on legacy. The main speed-skating venue located at the new Olympic Oval, just across the city limits in Richmond, is the more eye-catching and structurally daring of this new wave of buildings, but the Hillcrest curling centre provides an entirely different kind of problem-solving. The large volume, accommodating 6,000 spectator seats and one vast sheet of ice, is missing a number of floor plates, causing doorways to open halfway up vertiginous walls. The positions of future columns are marked out on the floor. 'In Olympic mode it's a clear span building; but in legacy mode it is subdivided and becomes a very different place. I think this is an extremely sensible way of building an Olympic facility,' says Condon. There are, however, sacrifices to the Olympic juggernaut: the large trusses ensuring a column-free space will appear to be unnecessary when walls are eventually placed beneath them; and at more than 10 metres (32.8-feet) high, required for camera angles and to create distance between broadcast standard lighting and the ice, this future community centre will appear a trifle larger than necessary. But when a building to has had two distinct lives within a year of completion, it can be forgiven the occasional anomaly.

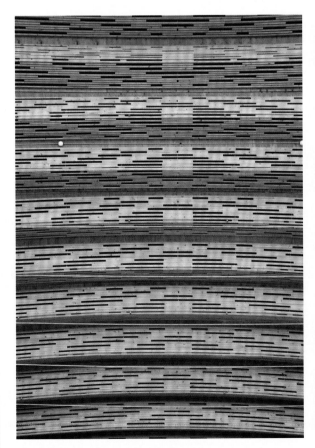

Wave-like forms of 2x4 timbers are located between the primary structural elements of the Oval's roof, providing a textured soffit and an acoustic baffle.

Interior of the Richmond Oval. Banks of temporary seating will enable the building to accommodate 8,000 spectators. Timber has been sourced from beetle-damaged trees.

Apart from keeping an eye on legacy, Vancouver's officials have also been pioneering new uses for British Columbia's principal natural resource – timber. It is something of a surprise to discover that a province famous for Douglas fir and western red cedar has tended to overlook timber as a construction material in favour of concrete and steel. Fears over fire safety and a general suspicion of timber's structural integrity means that buildings more than four storeys high cannot be constructed from wood. This, combined with ecological worries, has ensured that most of BC's timber products are exported to the US for low-rise 'stick-built' housing. Stringent forestry codes, including a particular sensitivity to the needs of wildlife and the avoidance of seeding monocultures, have helped rehabilitate timber as a building material, while officials have come to give architects the benefit of the doubt in fire and structural matters. 'We are a wood culture in British Columbia; wood is an important part of representing the place and our time. Also, people respond to timber very well,' says Condon.

Vancouver's new Convention and Exhibition Centre (actually a 102,000-square-metre (1.1 million-square-foot) 'west wing' to the original centre completed in 1986) certainly incorporates far more timber than would normally be the case. Functioning as the principal media centre for the Games, this steel and concrete building is merely fitted out in timber, but even that involved equipping the centre with two entirely separate sprinkler systems and a further facility to pump this coastal building full of seawater. Once permission to embark on a timber fit-out was granted, the architects (US firm LMN supported by local practices Downs/Archambault & Partners and the MCM Partnership) created the impression of a lumberyard – a million pieces of hemlock, structurally useless but fine for decorative effects, organised in 11 distinct compositions or 'families'. With the end grain running north–south throughout the building, and the long grain organised east–west, these timber wall surfaces add a warmth and texture that is conspicuously absent from other buildings of this type.

The speed-skating rink shares this visual warmth. And with a roof spanning 100 metres (328 feet), the building boasts some of the largest glulam members in the world. 'We're gradually eroding the preconception that timber is inherently dangerous,' says Larry Podhora, Vice-President of architects

LMN with Downs/Archambault & Partners and the MCM Partnership, Vancouver Convention and Exhibition Centre, Vancouver, 2008
Interior volumes have been clad in hemlock, deliberately reminiscent of a 'lumberyard'. It is highly unusual for so much timber to be present in large public buildings in British Columbia.

Walter Francl Architecture, Trout Lake Arena, Vancouver, 2009
Built as a community facility, the building will function as a practice space during the Olympics. Glulam beams rest on a steel beam that runs the length of the arena, creating a central clerestory.

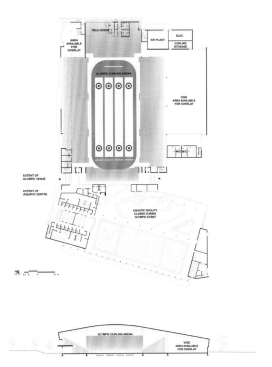

Plan and section of the curling centre in Olympic mode. The shaded areas indicate temporary seating.

Hughes Condon Marler Architects, Olympic curling venue, Hillcrest Park, Vancouver, 2009–10
Interior of the curling centre, only 'half built' before being completed for its legacy mode. Doors appear high up in walls; the patch in the foreground indicates the position of a future column.

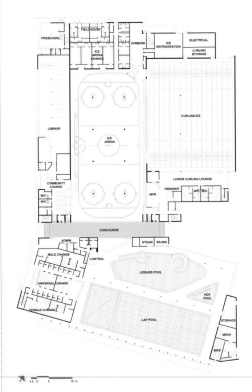

Plan of the curling centre in its post-Olympic form. An adjacent swimming centre will be brought into service, while the Olympic spaces will be subdivided for community use.

Canon Design. 'There are things that can be done with wood that we're only scratching the surface of.' These large spans are not constructed entirely of timber, in fact, but rely partly on the strength of steel – pure timber structures would have been ridiculously deep. What is clever, however, is that the timber has been engineered to contain many of the M&E services and air-handling ducts, while lengths of what Podhora calls 'the humble 2x4' have been marshalled in vast numbers to form an undulating soffit containing noise-attenuating fabric. Moreover, most of the timber on show has been harvested from Douglas fir trees damaged by the pine beetle, which causes death and discoloration in trees, although the structural integrity of the timber is unaffected.

This building is the only one of the 2010 Games' buildings that feels too large to ever be described as a 'community' facility; but it, too, is designed for subdivision, although jets of air will create distinct zones rather than solid walls. Completed in October 2008, the building proved popular long before the Olympics came to town, and the arrival of the Games will have been a temporary diversion in the recent history of this generous space. The city of Vancouver contains other, smaller, examples of this overall approach – buildings which meet genuine civic need and offer something of a local identity while remaining adaptable enough for the demands of global events. It is a model that has required much planning and confidence, but while it is too early to tell if legacy conditions will be met in the very long term, the signs are that Canada is providing a lesson that London's officials will do well to learn. Δ+

David Littlefield is a senior lecturer at the University of the West of England. He has written and edited a number of books, including *Architectural Voices: Listening to Old Buildings* (2007) and *Liverpool One: Remaking a City Centre* (2009), both published by John Wiley & Sons Ltd. He was also the curator of the exhibition 'Unseen Hands: 100 Years of Structural Engineering', which ran at the Victoria & Albert Museum in 2008.

FRANCIS-JONES MOREHEN THORP (FJMT)

The output of FJMT varies greatly in scale and location. The practice has completed community schemes in Sydney's suburbs as well as accommodation for prestigious institutions in the city centre. It has adapted existing structures on heritage sites as well as producing high-tech newbuilds. As **Fleur Watson and Martyn Hook** explain, what FJMT's projects have in common is an unwavering commitment to the enhancement of the public realm. The firm embraces the full responsibility of building in the sensitive urban and topographic context of this harbour city with its ridges and coastal inlets.

FJMT Design Director Richard Francis-Jones (left) with Managing Director Jeff Morehen (right).

The Sydney Opera House is arguably the most nation-defining example of Modern architecture in the Western world. Recently celebrating its 36th birthday, the building's sweeping iconic form is synonymous with Australia – a potent symbol of the 'lucky country' used in advertising campaigns, tourism merchandising and, perhaps most memorably, the logo of the 2000 Sydney Olympic Games bid. For Australian architects, it provides a striking reminder of the power of inspired public architecture to connect people to place. Jørn Utzon's masterpiece is clearly visible from the Circular Quay-based studio of architects Francis-Jones Morehen Thorp (FJMT) and Design Director Richard Francis-Jones describes it as much more than a national symbol: 'The Opera House is an incredible interpretation of its site. Its platform extends the rock of Bennelong out into the harbour as the great shell rises up over the water, creating a truly remarkable sculptural architecture,' he explains. 'Architecturally the most resonant aspects of the building lie in its tectonic depth and assembly along with the complete integration of form, structure, construction, materials and interpretation of landform … However, for me, the most important lesson that the Opera House has taught – and continues to teach – Australian architects lies in the creation of an uncompromisingly public place.'

Francis-Jones's position on the Opera House underwrites his belief that an investment in exceptional public architecture can create vital opportunities for growing Australian cities to effectively forge new relationships with key sites that when originally conceived were more concerned with pioneering growth than creating good places and civic spaces. It is a position that recalls a distinctly European origin and reveals the early influences that underpin the ethos of the practice. FJMT emerged as a result of working within the office of Mitchell/ Giurgola & Thorp (MGT), the award-winning practice that produced Australia's new Parliament House in Canberra (1988) among many other significant public buildings. MGT proved to be an influential teaching office where the Italian-born principal, Romaldo Giurgola, imbued the practice with his concern for light and space and an ongoing preoccupation with the legacy and philosophy of Louis Kahn. Giurgola believed in the power of public architecture to define the maturing nation of Australia and his influence lies at the heart of what Francis-Jones describes as 'FJMT's core agenda and commitment to the enhancement of the public realm'.

The Mint, Sydney, 2004
A fine assemblage composition of new buildings adds to the composition of historic sandstone buildings that were formerly Sydney's Mint. Redeveloped as the headquarters of the Historic Houses Trust, the new elements are sympathetic in scale and material to the original building yet provocative in activating new ways of using the collection of external spaces. The project seeks to redefine the manner in which historic architecture might be utilised in a sympathetic manner and restored without the pressure or compromise of reproduction.

Juxtaposition of old and new elements.

View across the central court by night.

Unlike many well-known architects or large-scale offices in Australia, FJMT did not follow the usual practice pathway by designing backyard renovations before progressing to bespoke housing, apartment buildings and eventually securing large-scale commercial or civic commissions. Emerging from the office and seminal influence of MGT, the practice was restructured in 2003 as FJMT and quickly secured large-scale commissions with projects at each major university in Sydney, sophisticated commercial buildings and residential developments along with detailed urban masterplans. However, it is through an investment in public architecture that Francis-Jones feels the agenda of the practice is most engaged. 'It is not about scale,' he insists, 'we are interested in small and large projects. Our key interest is in public work and in projects where there is the opportunity to explore ways to expand the public realm – even if this is on a very modest scale.'

This practice mandate, coupled with Francis-Jones's own writings on the subject, expresses a real concern for the current state of Sydney's urbanism and a clear rejection of the 'corporatisation' of the city's architecture. He explains: 'Sydney is a sensitive urban and topographic landscape. It is not laid out in a simple and robust city grid, but related to the fingers of ridges and harbour inlets. This city requires great care and understanding from its architects – it is a great responsibility to build here.'

FJMT's sensitivity in responding to the inherent challenges and opportunities of Sydney is clearly articulated in the project known as The Mint, a rehabilitation of a cluster of heritage buildings to house the new head office for the Historic Houses Trust, completed in 2004. Here the architects carefully and with great dexterity curated the insertion of a complex set of programmatic requirements into an important part of Sydney's historic fabric. While for many European countries a building from the 1850s might be considered hardly worth retaining, for an Australian city it is absolutely vital. The Mint reveals FJMT's solution for a contemporary and adaptive reuse of heritage buildings without any trace of precious historicism. New architecture is used to compose the civic nature of the trust while core activities are extended into external courtyards and sheltered verandahs that are sympathetic in scale and material to the original building yet provocative in activating new ways of using the collection of external spaces.

Insertion of new elements within the building's traditional fabric.

However, it is beyond the city centre and into the Sydney's sprawling suburbs that FJMT's work confronts the most difficult challenges with contexts dominated by shopping centres, consumerism and infrastructure. The firm's Max Webber Library in Blacktown (2005) – deep in Sydney's western corridor – carves out a critically needed civic space from the emergent city's overwhelmingly commercial hub. As Francis-Jones explains, FJMT's approach to the project was motivated by the 'equal challenge to resist the domination of private interest and consumerism in our cites and the consequential dilution of the public domain'. The design consists of two strong formal elements: a solid terracotta-clad box that houses the functional part of the brief and acts as a firm buffer to the adjacent context, while a louvred glass box – elevated above the street by a brick base – contains the reading room and the public spaces of the building. The clarity and distinction of the overall composition projects a quiet, contemplative calm among the noise and surrounding mash of ill-considered car-park retail.

Max Webber Library, Blacktown, Sydney, 2005
Surrounded by the commercial architecture of a major shopping centre, the Max Webber Library defines a new sense of civic presence in a non-space. The composed formal geometry of two strong boxes – one terracotta and one glass – both contextualise the architecture and reveal the public activity within. A bold central staircase lifts the public up into the reading room and reference collection with a grand gesture reinforced by a finely crafted ceiling that states the substantial public status of this modest architecture.

View across
Civic Place.

Staircase up to the reading room
and reference collection.

The solid, terracotta-tiled form
adjacent to the glazed box.

Faculty of Law, University of Sydney, Camperdown, Sydney, 2009
A key insertion into the university's masterplan, the Faculty of Law completes a grand civic campus space. The project comprises four major elements: a bar of academic offices, a triangle extrusion of teaching spaces, and a subterranean library with an iconic light canon, all united through a carefully composed ground surface. The building's formal qualities are reinforced by the sophisticated facade systems that layer skins of glass and operable moulded plywood sunscreens.

View across the Eastern Avenue forecourt.

The external materiality of the library building is both contextual and tough in contrast to the interior which reveals a dramatic double-height volume over the reading area. The sculptural ceiling form delivers soft reflected light into the depth of the plan, hovering over the generous stair that beckons the visitor up into the reading space. Reflecting on the project, Francis-Jones muses: 'It's interesting that the most complex and seemingly restricted projects give the most innovative and creative outcomes. They challenge us, shake us up, deny preconception, and force questions about our approach. We need to view such projects with completely open minds, not rush our answers, and give room for intuition as we feel our way into the site and into the real aspirations behind the project.'

This is a reflection that can be as aptly applied to FJMT's design for the Surry Hills Library & Community Centre, completed in 2009. Undergoing rapid gentrification, the formerly tough inner-city suburb of Surry Hills, to the south of the Central Business District and adjacent to Sydney's infamous Kings Cross, presented the architects with the challenge of responding with a facility

that could provide a focal point for the increasingly dislocated original community without isolating the new demographic of the area. FJMT's key consideration was to devise a highly considered siting strategy for the new building, reinforced by creating a wonderful transparency to the interior from the newly created adjacent public square. The expansive glass facade of the finely articulated cube-like form reveals the content of the architecture yet also acts as a device to provide comfort and air for users through a clever growing system of environmental controls. The natural system of vegetation is matched by a mechanical system of louvres on the east facade that adjust through the course of the day. The building's straightforward plan is supported and reinforced by a direct section with a library located on the ground and lower-ground floors, community functions in the middle and topped with a childcare centre and delightful external play space.

Undoubtedly, The Mint, Max Webber Library and Surry Hills Library & Community Centre are all projects that have contributed to FJMT's reputation as a highly successful, ideas-driven practice with an agenda for strong public engagement and masterful resolution of

Detail of the triple-layered facade system.

tectonics within a tight urban setting. However, Francis-Jones suggests that work won simply by accumulated experience provides a very narrow platform for a growing practice.

He is highly supportive of the power of the architectural competition to produce good architecture and create new opportunities for practices: 'I think competitions are an integral element of the culture of architecture; in a sense they are an extension of the collective studios of our schools of architecture. The more public the competition – with proposals exhibited, published and debated – the greater the contribution to the wider culture of architecture.' He continues: 'From the very beginning of the practice, the majority of FJMT's work has been won via architectural design competition. It's a process that we really enjoy. Even when we don't win we have still explored ideas, experimented and developed the investigative nature of our work.'

Francis-Jones describes the international competition for the Law School at the University of Sydney as the most 'public competition process' that the practice has encountered, with each short-listed competitor presenting their proposal in a public auditorium with the jury, fellow competitors,

The internal stair that links the library's two levels.

Surry Hills Library & Community Centre, Surry Hills, Sydney, 2009
The regeneration of the gritty inner-Sydney suburb of Surry Hills provides an apt context
for the insertion of this community facility that attempts to facilitate the existing residents
along with the suburb's new occupants attracted by the area's gentrification. As a truly
community-focused facility it provides a library and public meeting spaces balanced with a
new childcare centre on top. Establishing its presence adjacent to an important local park
and major street, the architecture is both iconic and appropriate for its site.

The spiral stair connecting the library's ground and lower-ground levels.

stakeholders and the public present. Indeed, the Faculty of Law at the University of Sydney (2009) represents a significant evolution in FJMT's work. The project builds on the master plan the practice developed for the university in 2002 and allows the architects to complete a key component of that plan in connecting the depths of the campus into the surrounding fabric of Camperdown. The sheer scale of the building is such that the monumental quality common in most university work is eroded through necessity into a collection of three forms: an articulated bar that houses the academics, the primary teaching spaces composed in a stacked triangular block, and the submerged library registered above ground by an iconic light cannon. These elements are held together by a constructed ground plane of paving and steps that stitches the new building back into the campus and evokes projection beyond its immediate realm.

The academic bar extends to connect with existing buildings forming a bridge that frames the park outside the campus. The architecture is striking through its material engagement with the existing campus and the materiality of its environmental systems with vast walls of plywood screens adjusting throughout the diurnal shifts in the passage of the sun. The sophisticated manipulation of the ground plane and appropriate dialogue with the adjacent grand heritage

Operable louvres on the
Crown Street facade.

View from Crown
Street at dusk.

architecture allows the presence of a law precinct to reinforce the intended ideal of a civic contemporary campus.

Among the diverse collection of projects produced by FJMT and their sensitive response to individual site and context, it is the practice's consistently compelling technological resolution that provides some measure of commonality between the projects. The shading systems and environmental performance in Australia's unforgiving climate are paramount to FJMT's work yet it resists a fetishisation of technology that a European architect such as Renzo Piano or Norman Foster – both of whom have completed projects in Sydney in the past decade – might indulge. As Francis-Jones explains: 'The technology and, in particular, the layering of the enclosure, is of great importance to the collective work – layering the light, view and space of the interface of the interior and exterior.' He continues: 'We regularly explore new forms, materials and systems to achieve this, but we combine our contemporary preoccupations with a great interest in natural materials – wood, stone and glass – that are imbued with a kind of collective memory and can be felt and not just seen. We strive to make buildings that are uncompromisingly modern, but also, in a sense, ancient.'

It is this commitment to an investment in time – to think, to reflect and to respond – that imbues FJMT's projects with a sense of considered intent and positions the work

as significant within the public realm. Returning to the lessons of the Opera House and his admiration for Utzon's commitment in creating a dynamic public role for architecture in Australia, Francis-Jones recalls: 'Each day when I am in our Sydney studio, for a short time in the late afternoon, the shadow of the Harbour Bridge moves across the shells of the Opera House and they turn from white to a soft red in the evening light. Each time this happens it causes a pause in our work, and pauses like this are absolutely invaluable.' ∆+

Fleur Watson is a design journalist, curator and former Editor-in-Chief of Australian architecture and design publication MONUMENT. Most recently, she has been appointed Curator of the State of Design Festival, a government-funded initiative that recognises Melbourne as the leading design centre within Australia. She is also a Director of Something Together, a multidisciplinary studio that focuses on presenting architecture and design in an intelligent and accessible way through the framework of exhibitions, events and publications.

Martyn Hook is a director of iredale pedersen hook architects in Melbourne, and Course Leader of the Architecture Programme at RMIT University. He recently completed a PhD by Project at RMIT entitled 'The Act of Reflective Practice', which explored the manner in which individual value systems are able to be maintained in collaborative architectural practice. He has been Guest Professor at TU Wien, TU Innsbruck and Wismar, and Visiting Critic at the Bartlett School of Architecture, UCL, the Mackintosh School of Architecture, Glasgow, and the University of Brighton.

Text © 2010 John Wiley & Sons Ltd. Images: p 118 © FJMT; pp 119(t), 120–3, 124(b), 125 © John Gollings; p 124(t) © Andrew Chung/FJMT

EMERGENCE AND THE FORMS OF METABOLISM

Earlier this year, **Michael Weinstock** published a seminal book, *The Architecture of Emergence: The Evolution of Form in Nature and Civilisation*, which challenges established cultural and architectural histories. The conventional worldview is expanded by placing human development alongside ecological development: the history of cultural evolution and the production of cities are set in the context of processes and forms of the natural world. As well as providing a far-reaching thesis, Weinstock's book gives lucid and accessible explanations of the complex systems of the physical world. In this abridged extract from Chapter 5, Weinstock explains the dynamics of individual and collective metabolisms from which intelligence and social and spatial orders emerge.

Michael Weinstock

Humans and all other living beings emerge from and exist within the dynamic processes and phenomena of the natural world, and they have had and continue to have a profound effect upon it. All the forms of nature and all the forms of civilisation have 'architecture', an arrangement of material in space and over time that determines their shape, size, behaviour and duration, and how they come into being. D'Arcy Thompson argued that the morphology of living forms has a 'dynamical aspect, under which we deal with the interpretation, in terms of force, of the operations of Energy'.[1] Living forms construct and maintain themselves by the exchange of energy and material through their surfaces, and in doing so they excrete changed materials and energy back into the environment. Metabolism is the 'fire of life',[2] and its processes transform and transport energy through the interior of the living form. All metabolic processes cease without a constant source of energy, although most living forms are capable of storing some energy in chemicals to survive temporary fluctuations in supply.

There is a relationship between energy and the lifespan and body mass of living systems. Small organisms are typically more metabolically active than larger ones, and the larger the organism, the slower the metabolism. A fast life is a short life: 'The light that burns twice as bright burns half as long.'[3] Whatever the size or shape of a living form, they all must capture and transform energy from their environment, and transport it in fluids to every cell. These processes require surfaces and fluid transportation networks, and there are geometrical parameters in the branching networks of living forms that are constant across all scales, from microbes to the largest trees and animals. The rate of energy that flows through a metabolism determines other variables that scale in relation to mass, such as the rate of fluid flow and the cross-section of the aorta or phloem vessels, or the number of heart beats in a lifespan.

It has long been a mystery as to why so many biological phenomena, such as lifespan, heart beats and respiratory rates should be related to body mass by 3/4, 1/4 or minus 1/4 powers. The quantative model of West, Brown and Enquist rests on the development of an abstract mathematical model of the maximally efficient branching network for the distribution of metabolic products and fluids. It provides a theoretical logic for the scaling of metabolic rate, and many other morphological parameters, in relation to the mass of a living form. There are three constants in the model: first, the network branches in a hierarchical series to supply all parts of the living form, so that the branches are self-similar, reducing in cross-section and length by a constant ratio; second, the end points of the smallest branches are always the same size no matter what the size or species of the living form is; and third, the branching network minimises the time and energy used to distribute the fluids and metabolic products, and the metabolic rate of the whole living form scales at the 3/4 power of the body mass.

Since its first publication in 1997, the model developed by West, Brown and Enquist has been successfully tested with the available observational data for all living forms.

The metabolic scaling characteristics emerge from the parameters of branching networks in the vascular system of trees and in both the cardiovascular and respiratory system of mammals. The model applies to the whole system of an organism, and it is argued that it incorporates both structural and hydrodynamic constraints, and is capable of accurately predicting many other allometric variables that scale in relation to mass, such as the parameters of fluid flow and the related dimensions of the vessels, the maximum height of trees, and ecological patterns of distribution of plant populations and communities.[4] Recent investigations are focused on the application of this model to cities.

Ecological organisation emerges from the interaction of the metabolic processes of all the forms of life that co-exist within a territory or habitat. All species, including humans, have a range or spatial area from which they gather energy, and over which they have an effect. An individual tree, for example, is anatomically organised to support its three-dimensional array of leaves for its photosynthetic metabolism. It will modify the soil and the atmosphere of its local environment by its metabolic processes – the transpiration of water drawn up from the ground will modify the structure of the soil, and the water

vapour and gases excreted by the leaves will modify the temperature, humidity and oxygen content of the atmosphere. This in turn will affect the metabolism of other trees near to it, as will the shade it casts. The spatial pattern of a mature forest, the density and distribution of varying sizes and species of plants, emerges from the interaction of all the plant metabolisms within it. Furthermore, the collective effect of the totality of metabolic actions produces the environment that other species inhabit; the bacteria and fungi, the insects, birds and animals that co-exist with the forest and within it. The processes of multiple individual systems, each acting across a range of spatial and temporal scales, interacts with the soil and topography, with sunlight and climate, water and atmosphere, to construct an ecological system. The flow of energy and material through an ecological system is thus regulated by the collective metabolism of all the living forms within it, and over time the regime of natural selection within the ecological system may be modified. At a finer scale, populations of individual living forms have an effect on their local environment, and in doing so they modify their own 'niche'[5] within the larger ecological system. Their descendants inherit and extend that local environment, and over many generations this changes the local regime of 'fitness' and, consequently, the dynamics of natural selection.

Termite behaviour and orders of magnitude
Colonies can produce three-dimensional material forms that are typically five or more orders of magnitude larger than the individual; for example the termite *Macrotermes bellicosus*, each individual only a few millimetres long, produces a fully developed nest that is up to 10 metres (32.8 feet) high and 30 metres (98.4 feet) in radius. The nest constructions of wasps, bees, ants and termites exhibit a wide range of forms, but all of them provide a thermally and chemically regulated environment, so extending the suitable climatic range for the species and modifying the energy requirements and metabolic rates of its individuals.

Many living forms extend their metabolism by a material construction that reduces the load or stress on some aspects of their metabolic processes. Insect colonies have highly structured social organisations, with restricted reproductive roles for individuals, generations that overlap in time, collaborative care of the offspring, and in many cases morphological distinction or castes for specialised roles. The material forms of the constructions of social insects are spatially complex and exhibit collective metabolic processes that are dynamically regulated to a very fine degree over time. The complex material organisation emerges from the interaction of millions of simple actions of individuals, each with a very small set of innate behaviours or 'motor programmes' that are triggered by chemical, thermal or hygroscopic stimuli. Individuals have differing thresholds and degrees of response to these stimuli, and so collective intelligent behaviour emerges from millions of slightly different interactions with the fluctuating internal and external material and metabolic conditions.

The extended metabolism of insect colonies has a fixed spatial relationship to the territory over which they range, with the nest or hive tending to be more or less centrally located. Intelligence, spatial organisation and material artefacts emerge from the collective extension of metabolism of the social insects. Insect collectives continually modify and regulate their exterior environment, and over time modify their ecological niche, and so enhance their 'fitness' in that environment. The close interrelation between the extended metabolism of the collective and their environment changes the regime of natural selection in their favour. In insect collectives there are no individuals with a capacity for processing information, and no system for the flow of information to a dominant decision-making individual or group. Responses to internal and external changes emerge from the actions of individuals, so that behavioural complexity emerges at the organisational scale of the collective. The emergence of distributed intelligence, of social and spatial organisation, of collective and materially extended metabolism, is reinforced and developed by positive feedbacks acting across a range of spatial and temporal scales.

The metabolism and social organisation of the great apes determine a very different spatial relationship of their material constructions to the territory over which they range. In chimpanzees the collective group is typically up to a hundred individuals with a territory that is determined by the distribution of the fruit, leaves and herbs that they feed on. This may be as much as 35 square kilometres (13.5 square miles) of forest, and a very much greater area in more open and mixed habitats. The whole community moves across their territory in loose association, split into smaller subgroups of four or six individuals, but moving closer together at night and weaving branches and leafy twigs into either tree or ground nests that collectively are arranged in an approximately circular plan. Chimpanzees make and use tools, extracting honey or insects with twigs, breaking open nuts with rocks, and using leaves to sip water. It is observed that knowledge and expertise of nest construction, tool-making and use is passed down through generations, immature individuals learning by imitating older, more proficient adults. However, variations do exist between communities in different regions with different climates, and with differing food quantity and quality. This suggests a material 'culture'[6] that involves the social transmission of knowledge that modifies the inherited and genetically conserved responses to environmental stimuli.

Phyllotaxis
The arrangement of leaves on a twig or stem, phyllotaxis or leaf ordering, is significantly related to the avoidance of self-shading. Leaves spring from a twig or stem at more or less the same angle, but in sequence are rotated so that they are offset from each other.

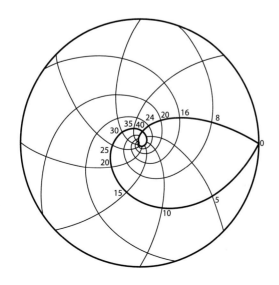

It is clear is that there are many similarities as well as differences between the dynamics of 'collectives' of the various taxa and species of apes and of insects. What is common between them is the large number of individuals with a range of different response thresholds, emerging from very small variations in the process of embryological development. Both positive and negative feedback occur in their interactions with each other and within their environment; in general, the gradation of responses across the population is either reinforced and accelerated by positive feedback, or inhibited by negative feedback. There is a high degree of redundancy in the relation of individuals to the collective, so that the numbers committed to specialised roles can be varied according to the circumstances – it is probable that this characteristic is also produced by the varied response thresholds of the multitude of individuals.

The relations of the spatial pattern of extended metabolic processes and material constructions are very different. The spatial pattern of the great apes arises from the ecological distribution and seasonality of food plants across the large defended territory of the group, and individuals move in loose association. Material constructions are temporary and individual, but closely grouped at night for defence. The spatial pattern of the social insects also arises from the ecological distribution of food plants, but the material construction tends to be centrally located in their territory, and is permanent. The evolution of human forms and culture involves both spatial patterns, extensive environmental modifications or 'niche construction' that is genetically conserved, and the emergence of a complex system for the transmission of knowledge over time. 𝄔+

Michael Weinstock, *The Architecture of Emergence: The Evolution of Form in Nature and Civilisation* (John Wiley & Sons, 2010), is available in paperback at £29.99 (PB ISBN: 978-0-470-06633-1) from www.wiley.com and www.Amazon.co.uk.

'Unit Factor' is edited by Michael Weinstock, who is Director of Research and Development and of Emergent Technologies and Design at the Architectural Association School of Architecture in London. He is co-guest-editor with Michael Hensel and Achim Menges of the *Emergence: Morphogenetic Design Strategies* (May 2004) and *Techniques and Technologies in Morphogenetic Design* (March 2006) issues of *Architectural Design*. He is currently writing a book on the architecture of emergence for John Wiley & Sons Ltd.

Notes
1. D'Arcy Thompson, 'Prologue', *On Growth And Form* (first published 1917), Cambridge University Press (Cambridge), 1961, p 19.
2. M Kleiber, 'Body size and metabolism', *Hilgardia* 6, 1932, pp 315–51.
3. '… and you have burned so very, very brightly, Roy.' From *Blade Runner*, 1982, directed by Ridley Scott, The Ladd Company, USA.
4. See BJ Enquist, 'Allometric scaling of plant energetics and population density', *Nature* 395, September 1998, pp 163–5; GB West, JH Brown and BJ Enquist, 'A general model for the origin of allometric scaling laws in biology', *Science* 276, 1997, pp 122–6; and DL Turcotte, JD Pelletier and WI Newman, 'Networks with side branching in biology', *Journal of Theoretical Biology* 193, August 1998, pp 577–92.
5. See KN Laland, FJ Odling-Smee and MW Feldman, 'The evolutionary consequences of niche construction: a theoretical investigation using two-locus theory', *Journal of Evolutionary Biology* 9: 1996, pp 293–316; and KN Laland, FJ Odling-Smee and MW Feldman, 'Niche construction, biological evolution and cultural change', *Behavioral and Brain Sciences* 23(1), 1999, pp 131–46.
6. See A Whiten, J Goodall, WC McGrew, T Nishida, V Reynolds, Y Sugiyama, CEG Tutin, RW Wrangham and C Boesch, 'Cultures in chimpanzees', *Nature* 399, 1999, pp 682–5; and A Whiten, V Horner and S Marshall-Pescini, 'Cultural panthropology', *Evolutionary Anthropology* 12, 2003, pp 92–105.

Metabolic scaling
The quantitative model of West, Brown and Enquist rests on the development of an abstract geometrical model of the maximally efficient branching network for the distribution of metabolic products and fluids. There are three constants in the model. One, the network branches in a hierarchical series to supply all parts of the living form, so that the branches are self-similar, reducing in cross-section and length by a constant ratio; Two, the end points of the smallest branches are always the same size no matter what the size or species of the living form is; Three, the branching network minimises the time and energy used to distribute the fluids and metabolic products, and the metabolic rate of the whole living form scales at the 3/4 power of the body mass.

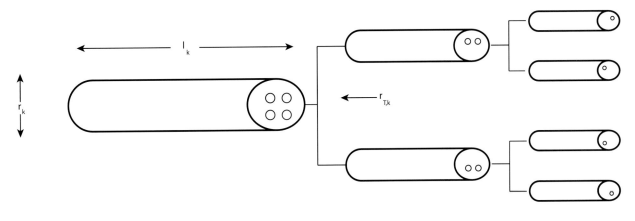

k=0   k=1   k=2

BIODIVERSITY TARGETS AS THE BASIS FOR GREEN DESIGN

Mike Wells, the Director of Biodiversity by Design, and **Ken Yeang** outline the need for biodiversity targets in architecture to provide a more far-reaching basis for green design. Rather than just literally 'greening' a building by covering it with foliage, they seek to encourage designers to engage with wider ecological processes and in more specific detail.

Ken Yeang

The next level of urban 'greening' must go beyond the mere introduction of soft landscape into and around built form. It must exceed the ecomimetic balancing of the abiotic (non-living) with biotic (living) constituents of built form and urban development, instead striving to produce buildings and urban areas as living habitats that are designed as functional ecosystems.[1]

The Utility of Biodiversity Versus Greening

Ecodesign should create linked ecological nexuses between vegetation on buildings, the green space between buildings and the vegetation of the surrounding habitat, but it must go beyond this. Designing for biodiversity, as opposed to just 'greening', can realistically, and should, entail the creation of excellent analogues of diverse natural or semi-natural habitats both nearby[2] and, indeed, on and within buildings, even right in the heart of a city.[3]

According to the International Convention on Biological Diversity, 'biodiversity' is 'the variability among living organisms from all sources including, inter alia, terrestrial, marine and other aquatic ecosystems and the ecological complexes of which they are part; this includes diversity within species, between species and of ecosystems.'[4] This definition indicates that designing for biodiversity has to be more than just the inclusion of a collection of plant species even if these are native to the locality. It requires designing with, and for, the locality's ecological systems, process and interactions, including their variation in space and time.

The value of biodiversity to humans can be assessed or measured in a variety of different ways. Simply stated, without properly functioning terrestrial and aquatic ecosystems the human species would almost certainly disappear. In a more local or specific context, biodiversity has different types and levels of utility. As regards survival of urban green infrastructure in the long term, the more complex food webs and ecosystems are, the more resilient they tend to be in the face of environmental perturbations. Environmental perturbations are predicted to increase in frequency and severity under the currently predicted climate change, and urban design must be made as resilient as possible to accommodate/ adapt to these changes.[5] More biodiverse and ecologically balanced terrestrial and aquatic systems also tend to stay healthier and require less expensive maintenance than monocultures.

However, benefits of diversity in urban greening can be more subtle. The adverse consequences of our human activities on our psychological health and well-being are often accentuated in our urban environments. For some time it has been known that we often show preferences for more bucolic scenes and that experience of greener, more natural environments can counteract these adverse psychological effects.[6] These benefits have been linked to decreased illness and absenteeism, and even increased productivity in the workplace. More recently it has been shown in the UK that more biodiverse environments are associated with greater human psychological health benefits and well-being than comparable but less biodiverse environments.[7]

Moral arguments regarding the inherent right to exist of the full range of non-human biodiversity are, to many, also pertinent to the concept of 'value'. And contrary to some earlier texts on urban ecology, real biological rarity can and does exist in urban areas.[8]

In essence, it could be said that while just greening is good, biodiverse-based greening is better. Enhancing a locality's biodiversity in urban design, especially (though not exclusively) with native biodiversity, has to be a key part of our design of new buildings, retrofitting existing stock, and in the creation of new urban environmental infrastructure for whole urban sectors.

Targets in Biodiverse Design

At the outset, advanced green design aims to create new habitats and sets biodiversity targets for each of the newly created habitats or ecosystems (and

1 Priority species for nature conservation
2 Flagship: species in this temperate mixed forest climate, that could symbolise scheme success

Indicator species/umbrella species that indicate healthy populations of supporting species and/or good semi-natural environmental conditions

3 Indicator of good populations of small mammals
4 Indicator of good populations of small birds
5 Indicator of good populations of fish/ amphibians
6 Indicator of good populations of invertebrates
7 Indicator of good water quality
8 Species with special aesthetic qualities or interest to man e.g. conspicuous beauty, song or tendency to use artificial refuges

KEY

- DPS — Dominant plant species
- WQ — Water quality
- AA — Approximate area
- (icon) — Pair Breeding
- F — Feeding

J F M A M J J A S O N D
Season which they occur- if full means resident

Biodiversity Target →
Target Species ↓

Target Species	Shrub Roofs (WQ Moderate, AA 1.6ha)	Grassland Roofs (WQ Moderate, AA 1.2ha)	Planted facades (WQ Moderate, AA 2ha)	Densely wooded area (WQ, AA 0.2ha)	Reeds and Settlement pond (WQ, AA 0.9ha)	Wet Woodland (WQ Moderate, AA 0.8ha)	Marsh (WQ High, AA 0.4ha)	Polishing Pond with Rafts (WQ High, AA 0.4ha)	Flowing Water and Still Ponds-Urban (WQ Very High, AA 0.3ha)	Streetscape Planting (WQ Moderate-low, AA 0.6ha)
Siberian Weasel *Mustela sibirica* 3,4				(weasel) F	F	PB F	F			
Shrews *Crocidura lasiura, Crocidura suaveolens* 6				(icon) F		PB F	PB F			
Rodents Several species				PB F	PB F	PB F	PB F			
Northern Bat *Eptesicus nilssonii* 6,8	F	F	F	(bat) F		F				F
Daubenton's Bat *Myotis daubentonii* 6,7,8				(bat) F		F	PB	F	F	
Big-footed Myotis *Myotis macrodactylus* 6,8			(bats)					F	F	
Moorhen *Gallinula chloropus* 8					PB F		F	PB F	PB F	
Eastern Spot-billed Duck *Anas zonorhyncha* 8								PB F	PB F	
Little Egret *Egretta garzetta* 2,5					F		F			
Eurasian Sparrowhawk *Accipter Nisus* 4,8	F		F	PB F		F				
Eurasian Kestrel *Falco tinnunculus* 3		F		F	F	F	F			
Oriental Turtle Dove *Streptopelia orientalis*	PB F		F	PB						PB F
Oriental Scops Owl *Otus sunia* 6,8	PB		F	PB F		F				F
Collared Scops Owl *Otus lettia* 6,8	PB	F	PB	PB F		F				F
Hoopoe *Upupa epops* 5,6,8		PB F		PB		F				
Pygmy Woodpecker *Yungipicus kizuki* 1,2	F			PB F		PB F				F
Brown Shrike *Lanius cristatus*	PB F			PB F	F	PB F	F			F
Eurasian Siskin *Carduelis spinus*	F				F					
Azure-winged Magpie *Cyanopica cyanus* 6	F	F		PB F		PB F				F
Brown-eared Bulbul *Microscelis amaurotis*	PB F		F	PB F		PB F				
Oriental Reed Warbler *Acrocephalus orientalis* 2,6,8					PB F	F	F			
Black-browed Reed Warbler *Acrocephalus bistriciceps* 8					PB F					
Chinese Penduline Tit *Remiz consobrinus* 2,6,7						F	F	F	F	
Red-rumped Swallow *Cecropis daurica* 6	F	F	PB	F	F	F	F	F	F	F
Dybowski's Frog *Rana dybowski* 2,6					(frog) F	F	F			
Dark-spotted Frog *Pelophylax nirgomaculatus* 6					(frog) F	F	F	(frog) F	F	
Dragonflies 20+ species 1,2,7	F	F	F	F	(dragonfly) F		(dragonfly)	(dragonfly)	(dragonfly) F	
Yellow-tip *Anthocharis scolymus* 8	F			(butterfly) F			(butterfly) F			(butterfly) F
Scarce Heath *Coenonympha hero* 6	(butterfly) F		F	F	F		(butterfly) F	F		(butterfly) F

Densely wooded area DPS: *Salix pseudo-lasiogyne, Carodiphyllum japonicum, Lagerstroemia indica, Prunus glandulosa, Celtis sinensis, Iridaceae pseudoacorna*

Reeds and Settlement pond DPS: *Phragmites australis, Iridaceae pseudoacorus, Iris koreana*

Wet Woodland DPS: *Alnus hirsuta, Alnus japonica, Salix koreensis, Salix purpurea Var japonica, Crataegus pinnatifida, Rosa koreana, Rosa maximoviciziana*

Marsh DPS: *Equisetum palustre, Sparganium erectum, Imperata cylindrica, Setaria viridis, Acorus gramineus, Hypericum erectum, Caltha palustris*

Polishing Pond with Rafts DPS: *Phragmites australis, Iridaceae pseudoacorus, Iris koreana, Hypericum erectum, Caltha palustris*

Flowing Water and Still Ponds-Urban DPS: *Iridaceae pseudoacorus, Iris koreana, Nymphoides peltata, Nuphar japonicum, Utricularia japonica*

Streetscape Planting DPS: *Prunus Yedoensis matsum, Styrax japonica, Cornus officinalis, Prunus mume, Lagerstroemia indica, Lysoria radiata, Oenothera odorata, Lychnis fulgens*

Landscape and architectural biodiversity habitats and targets for Geyong-gi New City, Seoul, South Korea. The different columns separate the different sub-areas/habitats being proposed (the small plans showing thir intended locations) and the rows show the target species or species groups. The location-specific targets are shown in the cells of the table.

there could be several on or around a given building) and determines ways to achieve these targets over the life of the built development. Such biodiversity targets reflect specific design objectives and not just a general concept with the intention of 'greening'. Setting targets can help ensure a better, more functional and more sustainable green infrastructure that survives over the long term, thereby achieving better integration of the natural and the man-made.

We can set biodiversity targets at many levels and in relation to as many ecosystem properties as is feasible within available knowledge and budget. While we can now, in principle, green our cities with a continuous 'ecoinfrastructure' (for example, using 'ecobridges' and 'ecoundercrofts'),[9] we need to further prescribe its intended ecological functions and measure its ecological success.

Biodiversity target-setting is complex and will necessarily be incomplete and based to a greater or lesser extent on assumptions. Lack of full data, however, does not invalidate the process of setting and using targets. It is also certainly true that not setting targets from the beginning greatly reduces a project's chances of achieving sustainable multifunctionality of design.

At present, incorporating biodiversity targets in our architectural designs has not widely taken place and multifunctional or even spatial or experiential greening goals have rarely been systematically set in advance in designing our built environment.

The criteria for biodiversity targets should be 'SMART': specific, measurable, achievable, realistic and time-scaled. The presence or absence of a feature can be a target, whether introduced directly or attracted to the built form. However, target utility in improving a design's quality increases if predictions of quantity can be made, for example numbers or extent at different times of the year or day. This requires sufficient knowledge of the locality's species/habitat biology, and so biodiversity targets need not necessarily always be based on the rarest species examples.

The basis for setting a given species in the design's set of biodiversity targets could include those that are, for example:

- 'priority' species – to the wider nature conservation targets of a given area;

- 'keystone' species – having a disproportionate effect in terms of the functioning of the local environment (one example might be several species of bee that are in global decline, their potential loss being a threat to agriculture everywhere);

- 'flagship' species – those that champion the biodiversity of the sites in question, often because of their conspicuousness, impressive appearance or cultural iconography;

- 'umbrella' species – useful in making conservation-related decisions, typically because protecting these indirectly protects a wider variety of species and faunal/floral communities;

- 'indicator' species – for example, those at the top of the food chain where the effects of environmental pollution accumulation and toxicity can be first apparent, warning us about threats to our own health; or

- 'healing' species – for example, species of bird with particularly melodious song or perhaps a plant with a particularly appealing perfume.

A matrix can be prepared showing species identification and biodiversity targets (see the one here, which focuses on certain fauna that may utilise a proposed development. In this case the targets are only at the masterplan level of detail; at a later design stage many would be quantified, for example the actual numbers of pairs of nesting birds or sizes of likely flocks would be added as targets). Furthermore, 'negative' targets can also be defined and identified, for example the absence of certain alien invasive species (the presence of which is often symptomatic of bad ecosystem and landscape design). A very useful array of potential metrics that could be associated with targets for biodiversity in urban design has just been developed by the Singapore National Parks Board, and a user guide to it published in draft form.[10]

Biodiversity targets can and should also be set for various measures of the ecosystem's health and/or the conservation status of a species population. Targets should be as specific as biotic or abiotic data allow. For example, for a 0.2 hectare (0.49-acre) urban reed bed in a wetland mosaic in London: 'Presence of at least two pairs of breeding Reed Warblers in the majority of the year over the first ten years of monitoring. Nest hatching and fledging rates to be at or above the south of England urban average for the species.' A target such as this could indicate the presence of a healthy reedbed system (of a given size), with an appropriate complementary adjacent ecosystem development and appropriate management to prevent excessive human disturbance.

Part of the sward on the 3-hectare (7.4-acre) living roofs of the Moos lakewater filtration plant in Willishofen, Zurich. This sward is now the only remaining example of this grassland type in this canton of Switzerland and has been proposed as a national park. There are more than 175 plant species on the roof, among them seven orchid species, including around 6,000 green-winged orchids.

Living roof on the Rossetti Building of the Cantonal Hospital of Basel. The habitat is based on unusual riverine gravel grassland and is used by a diverse range of uncommon invertebrates and birds.

The designer also needs to ensure that the physical ecosystem parameters that underpin the various ecosystems of the locality should also be set as biodiversity targets as far as possible. These may include water quality parameters (for example, based on levels of available phosphorus, Secchi disc readings or chlorophyll measures),[11] or soils' nutrient status (soils over-rich in nutrients often support impoverished biodiversity).

Any of the above targets can be used as indicators of successful and balanced ecosystem function, with all the associated benefits that accompany ecosystem content and services.

As with any endeavour relating to natural systems, the designer needs to allow for the unexpected and the evolution of natural systems that may occur in unpredicted ways. Biodiversity targets are accordingly not the absolute criteria of a scheme's success or failure, but are to be regarded as clear ambitions for review in the light of habitat development and succession. These targets should be, to some extent, regarded flexibly – if ecosystem maturation indicates that new alternative goals might be more fruitfully pursued or be beneficial, we can revoke our initial targets and introduce modified or even new ones throughout a design's development and use.

In designing 'green' buildings or 'green' construction, we need to look further than simply the inclusion of green landscape in and around built form. We need to

create viable habitats within the design, and to set biodiversity targets for these habitats that are to be achieved over the life of the building or development. The above provides the framework for such an approach to ecodesign and the designing of green ecoinfrastructure in master plans, that goes beyond the inclusion of extensive vegetation, even if this consists mainly or entirely of native plant species, in the designed landscape. ⚙+

Mike Wells is a professional ecologist and a Visiting Research Fellow of the University of Bath School of Architecture and Civil Engineering where he has developed and taught a course entitled 'Ecology, Sustainability and the Architect' since 1999. He has also lectured on sustainable ecological urban design for the Cities Programme of the London School of Economics. He is the co-author of various guideline documents in ecological assessment and design practice, has worked internationally for the past 20 years as an ecological consultant, and is a founding director of Biodiversity by Design, an ecological consultancy based in Bath.

Ken Yeang is a director of Llewelyn Davies Yeang in London and TR Hamzah & Yeang, its sister company, in Kuala Lumpur, Malaysia. He is the author of many articles and books on sustainable design, including *Ecodesign: A Manual for Ecological Design* (Wiley-Academy, 2006).

Notes
1. See K Yeang, *Ecodesign: A Manual for Ecological Design*, John Wiley & Sons (London), 2006.
2. See MJ Wells, 'Ecologically-led landscape design in brownfield regeneration projects', in *Proceedings of the 16th Conference of the Institute of Ecology and Environmental Management: Designing Nature into Urban Development and Regeneration*, IEEM (Winchester), 2006.
3. MJ Wells and G Grant, 'Biodiverse vegetated architecture worldwide: status, research and advances', in *Proceedings of the 22nd Conference of the Institute of Ecology and Environmental Management: Sustainable New Housing and Major Developments – Rising to the Ecological Challenges*, IEEM (Winchester), 2006.
4. International Convention on Biological Diversity: www.cbd.int/convention/convention.shtml.
5. See N Stern, *The Economics of Climate Change*, Cambridge University Press (Cambridge), 2007.
6. See CLE Rhode and AD Kendle, *Human Well-Being, Natural Landscapes and Wildlife in Urban Areas: A Review*, English Nature (Peterborough), 1994; See RS Ulrich, R Simons, Bd Losito, E Fiorito, M Miles and M Zelson, 'Stress recovery during exposure to natural and urban environments, *Journal of Experimental Psychology* 11, 1991, pp 201–30; RS Ulrich, 'Effects of gardens on health outcomes: theory and research', in CC Marcus and M Barnes (eds), *Healing Gardens*, Wiley (New York), 1999, pp 27–86; and A Burls and W Caan, 'Human Health and Nature Conservation', *British Medical Journal* 331, 2005, pp 1221–22.
7. RA Fuller, KN Irvine, P Devine-Wright, PH Warren and KJ Gaston, 'Psychological benefits of greenspace increase with biodiversity', *Biological Letters* 5, 2007, pp 352–5.
8. G Kadas, 'Rare invertebrates colonizing green roofs in London', *Urban Habitats* 4(1), 2005, pp 66–86.
9. K Yeang, *Ken Yeang: Ecomasterplanning*, John Wiley & Sons (London), 2009.
10. Singapore National Parks Board, 'User's manual for the Singapore Index on Cities' Biodiversity', 2009. See http://www.cbd.int/doc/groups/cities/cities-draft-user-manual-singapore-index-2009-07-01-en.pdf.
11. MJ Wells, M Luszczak and B Dunlop, 'Sustainable habitat creation in Nottingham on a former industrial site', in HR Fox, HM Moore and AD McIntosh (eds), *Land Reclamation: Achieving Sustainable Benefits*, AA Balkema (Rotterdam/Brookfield), 1998, pp 143–55.

Neil Spiller

'Significant changes in cultural
paradigms, global dynamics
and the practice of architecture
suggest that versatility and
conceptual broadening may
be a viable alternative to
increasingly dominant forms of
specialisation and "schematic"
spatial production – method
breadth is crucial toward this
possibility,' writes Kulper.

STRATEGIC PLOTS AND SPATIAL BLOOMS

Stifled by 'architect's block'? Reached an
insurmountable creative impasse? **Neil Spiller** directs
us back to that old stalwart the drawing; and in so
doing introduces the inspiring output of Perry Kulper,
'the Michigan Magus', which 'provokes the mind into
tangents, to ambitions and delightful juxtapositions
not only of forms but also of ideas'.

Perry Kulper,
Metaspheric
Zoo, 2005.

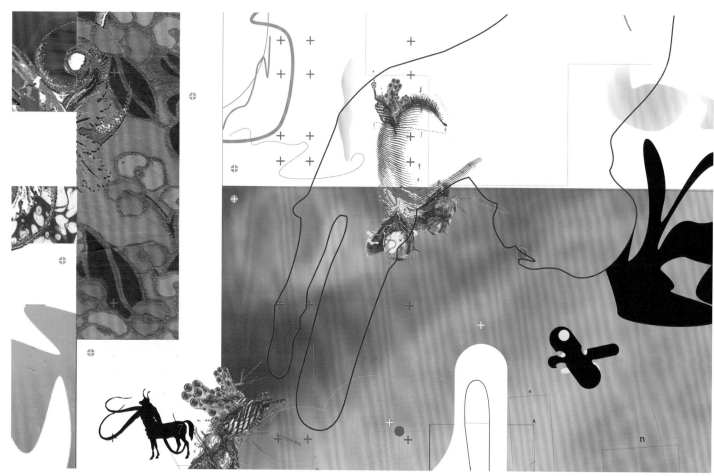

We all know the feeling; you've been introduced to a new project through a client, through a competition brief, through a tutor, or have invented a self-set architectural problem to solve. You pick up the pencil or pen, you start to make a few wobbly marks, the old muse hasn't returned. The problem seems insurmountable, impossible, but somehow you must crack its husk. Or have you really met your match? Is your career to date just hype over substance, like all the other architects who are your rivals? Only you have seen the true potential of contemporary architecture, only you will know what to do, if only you could break the stranglehold of the current circumstances and its formal prisons. Familiar phrases such as 'putting a quart into a pint pot' come to mind. Sketch after sketch, some drawings on the site plan are discarded, thrown away, torn up. You walk up and down the street: coffee, cigarettes, music, and a quick look at some of your heroes' books – but nothing. Despair and loss of confidence follow – you walk away, leave it, come back to it later.

Perry Kulper,
Metaspheric
Zoo, 2005

What is happening here? This is the rickety creative process, this is the conscious mind reaching out to the subconscious mind. This is the creative process sifting H-creative and P-creative ideas and concepts. P-creative ideas are the ones that are new ideas to you personally; they are not necessarily entirely original, but if you dress them up in all your usual architectural lexicon, people rarely notice. H-creative notions are the ones that you really want. These are ideas that are historically original, like Einstein's or Darwin's. Such ideas are great epistemological shifts, discontinuities in human culture.

It is the vicissitudes of the drawing, the act of drawing and the re-evaluation of these drawings that help us architects ground our work as a series of material juxtapositions, site placements and programmatic syntheses. So the drawing is a kind of shamanistic goad; it is through the drawing's rhythms that we are lulled into a creative trance and it is through the drawing that we navigate through our landscape of trials, tribulations and creative peaks. A few years ago I described the drawing thus:

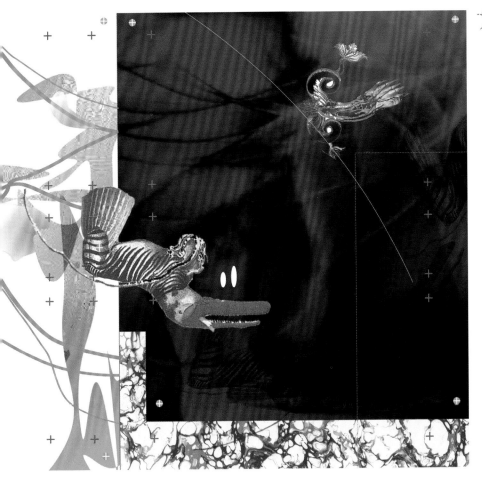

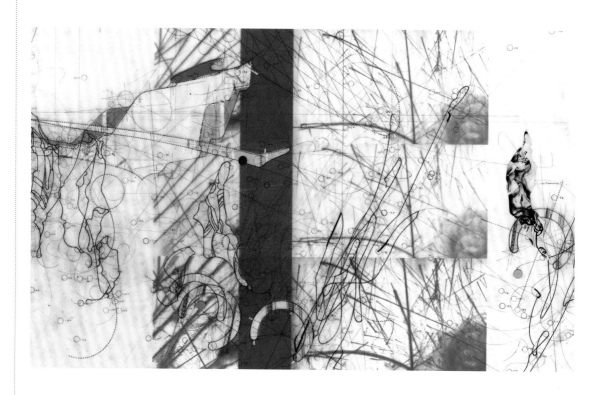

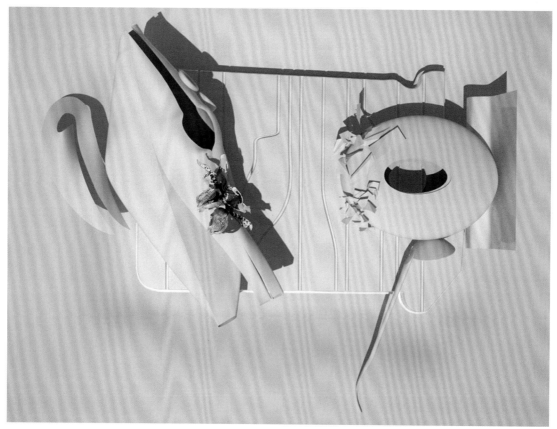

Perry Kulper, Central
California History
Museum, Fresno,
California, 2002

The drawing is a way of primitively recording the body's creative trance; it is akin to a ritualistic shaman's dance that unveils a journey into the realm of the gods. The architectural secret is a secret even to its creator at this early stage. The result is a drawn text containing allegorical marks defining the complex physical and emotional context in which it is drawn. Contrary to popular belief, architecture on paper is not safe; it is a place where secrets are either told or kept. Such drawings are personal cartography, a map of intentions on a quest for creative identity. The conditions of society, site and drawing meet as the architect becomes a social and personal condenser, with the drawing a mixing-desk for secret music.[1]

I was very much reminded of these thoughts recently when listening to my friend Perry Kulper giving a lecture. Perry, the Michigan Magus, draws the most exquisite work of this particular architectural niche. His work provokes the mind into tangents, to ambitions and delightful juxtapositions not only of forms but also of ideas. His work is 'mental chewing gum', in the nicest sense of the phrase. It inspires the reader with something to grapple with; something always sticks and something is always morphed into new relationships. I leave you with some of his thoughts on the drawing:

The drawing is a virtual machine and ours a shot gun marriage to it … Her, his or their "accomplice", the drawing operates at the clogged intersection of circumstance, cultural import and creative identity. Like an enigmatic and mysterious sea (which forgets and remembers at the same time), the space of the drawing is at times a wild and untamed medium. On the one hand, it provides moments of coordination and lost wanderings of the creative mind … an alchemic cauldron for untold and emergent stories all in a quest for meaningful engagement and psychological metamorphosis with the world.[2]

So, with this inspiration – get chewing! △+

Neil Spiller is Professor of Architecture and Digital Theory, Director of Graduate Design and Vice Dean at the Bartlett School of Architecture, University College London.

Notes
1. Neil Spiller, *Digital Dreams: Architecture and the New Alchemic Technologies*, Ellipsis (London), 1998, p 19.
2. Perry Kulper, Unpublished lecture, Bartlett School of Architecture, University College London, 7 October 2009.

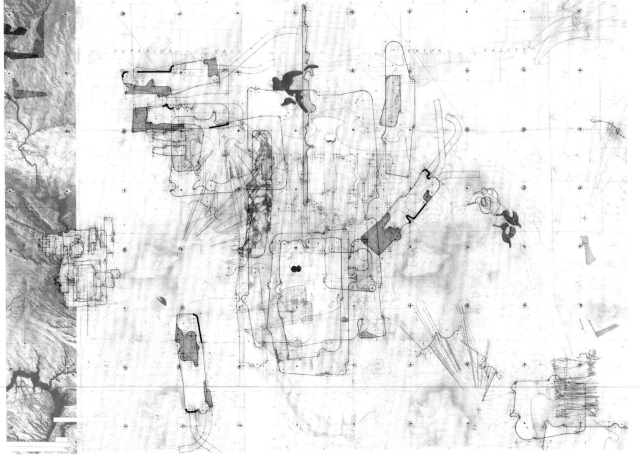

Perry Kulper, Fast Twitch: Desert Dwelling, 2004.

Nuggets

now with added holes

new nuggets 20% less ink

Sample of Utrecht-based communications firm Spranq's Ecofont®.

Holey

In a waste-saving exercise, Dutch marketing company Spranq[1] has launched a modified typeface, Ecofont®, which uses significantly less ink by incorporating holes into the design of individual characters, without any significant effect on legibility. As reported in *National Geographic*,[2] a fifth of a 10-point character could remain unprinted yet remain readable. This raises the question as to how much of any given material can be removed while maintaining its material and/or structural integrity. The confectionery industry has been perfecting this for years with any number of aerated profit-enhancing edible substrates; similarly in structural design we start with a beam, then we put holes in it (castellating), then we add more air by creating a truss and so on. Even in the heavyweight world of reinforced concrete, products such as Bubbledeck[3] and Cobiax[4] can significantly reduce the dead load (by up to 35 per cent) and thus the relative strength of a slab by introducing holes (hollow plastic spheres, actually) to the (concrete) mix. Meanwhile, foamed metals such as foamed aluminium (which looks much like it sounds) continue to promise more than their thus far limited construction applications suggest. A neat example of the designed and engineered removal of material, in this case stainless-steel sheet, is Niall McLaughlin's Mead's Reach footbridge in Bristol (2008). Working in collaboration with the Price and Myers Geometrics group, the finite element analysis (FEA) of the design has been mapped directly on to this stressed skin structure by the selective and variable radii laser-cut perforations covering the 55-metre (180-foot) longstructure.

Synaesthetic

A recent article in *Scientific America* reports the forthcoming release of BrainPort, a new cross-sensory device (or aid) designed to enable its visually impaired users to 'partially restore the experience of seeing'.[5] An eyeglass-mounted miniature camera is connected to a small handheld computer that translates digital images into electrical pulses, which unexpectedly are fed back on to a small electrode array that sits on your tongue. The late neuroscientist Paul Bach-Y-Rita, who inspired the invention of the device, stated: 'We see with our brains not our eyes.'[6] So while not restoring sight, BrainPort will provide additional spatial orientation information through what is described as 'a sensory substitution technique'. If this interchangeable set of sensory inputs and outputs seems improbable, then what about the more complex sensory wiring and cognitive design of the synaesthete?

For a fascinating and readable description of synaesthetic ability see AR Luria's *The Mind of a Mnemonist*,[7] a book that renowned neurologist and author Oliver Sacks said he thought was a work of fiction, but was actually 'a wonderful case history, with the accuracy of science, but all the sensibility, drama and structure of a novel'.[8] Luria dedicates a small section of his book to his patients' synaesthetic abilities, which are explored by playing sounds with variable frequencies (pitch in hertz) and amplitude (volume). On hearing certain frequencies, the patient (named 'S' in the book) can specifically describe colour, shape, movement and, in some cases, taste:

Presented with a tone pitched at 2000 Hz and having an amplitude of 113 dB (admittedly quite loud!) S said: 'It looks something like fireworks tinged with a pink-red hue. The strip of colour feels rough and unpleasant, and it has an ugly taste – rather like that of a briny pickle … You could hurt your hand on this.'[9]

In Richard Cytowic's comprehensive, but possibly less poetic book *Synesthesia*,[10] he sets out an impressive body of research to lift the subject out of the esoteric and establishes the study of synaesthesia and the synaesthete as a fascinating branch of evidenced neuropsychology. In his second edition of 2002, many of the more evocative case studies or accounts of synaesthesia and art are omitted, but painter David Hockney – who Cytowic examined personally in 1981– is classified as having the synaesthetic ability of coloured hearing.

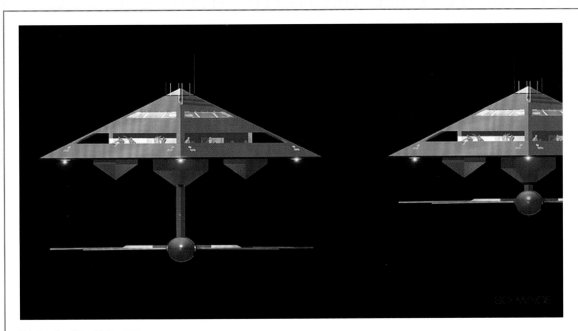

Schwinge Associates, Trinity HYSWAS
Tetrahedron Motor Yacht, 2009.

Tetrafacts

While pondering the inherent structural instability of a cube (or at least its framework), its obvious lack of cross-bracing or triangulation is clearly the cause. By diagonally traversing each of the six sides with a strut or cable, you also describe the six vertices of that most structurally stable of plutonic solids: the four-faced tetrahedron. So why is architecture so enamoured with the 90-degree connections of the wobbly cube? Which is just what Richard Buckminster Fuller asked and demonstrated, both theoretically and practically, with designs such as his octet truss (an isotropic vector matrix) based on the close packing of spheres. Fuller also declared that the almost magic tetrahedron could stretch the credulity of ordinary maths and stated: 'When we take two triangles and add one to the other to make the tetrahedron, we find that one plus one equals four.'[11] So from two triangles with six vertices between them we get a four-faced object described with the same six edges. Buckminster Fuller claimed that this was not just some geometric trickery, but that chemistry and chemical bonding utilise similar principles. Is it merely coincidental that when synaesthete 'S' in Luria's *The Mind of a Mnemonist* is asked to describe his synaesthetic response to a series of numbers, the number three is 'a pointed segment, that rotates'[12] (which sounds fairly dynamic), whereas the number four (surely the close two-dimensional relative of the cube) is 'square and dull'.[13] Exemplars of tetrahedral artefacts include Ruben Rausing's billion-dollar business starter, the original four-faced milk carton the Tetra Pak (now the Tetra Classic Aseptic) and Alexander Graham Bell's man carrying tetrahedral kites from the late 19th and early 20th centuries, brilliantly described and illustrated in David Pelham's book *Kites*.[14] More recently, architect Jonathan Schwinge's proposed Trinity Tetrahedron Motor Yacht[15] uses a HYSWAS[16] hull to lift the purely tetrahedral superstructure out of the water when in motion, creating the effect of a levitating platonic solid moving at some not inconsiderable speed above the water line. Δ+

'McLean's Nuggets' is an ongoing technical series inspired by Will McLean and Samantha Hardingham's enthusiasm for back issues of *AD*, as explicitly explored in Hardingham's *AD* issue *The 1970s is Here and Now* (March/April 2005).

Will McLean is joint coordinator of technical studies (with Pete Silver) in the Department of Architecture at the University of Westminster. He recently co-authored, also with Pete Silver, the book *Introduction to Architectural Technology* (Laurence King, 2008), and is currently co-authoring a book on structures, with Silver, due for publication in 2011.

Notes

1. www.spranq.nl/en/.
2. J Berlin, 'Environment: Holey Grail', *National Geographic*, August 2009, p 16.
3. www.bubbledeck.com.
4. www.cobiax.ch/.
5. M Kendrick, 'Tasting the Light', *Scientific America*, October 2009, pp 22–4.
6. See http://host.madison.com/news/article_30367b45-5a90-50d4-beed-ebf98df7f8cf.html.
7. AR Luria, *The Mind of a Mnemonist*, Penguin Books (London), 1975.
8. See http://luria.ucsd.edu/Luria.mov.
9. Luria, op cit, p 25.
10. RE Cytowic, *Synesthesia: A Union of the Senses*, MIT Press (Cambridge, MA), 2002.
11. R Buckminster Fuller, *Synergetics*, Macmillian Publishing (New York), 1982, pp 8–9.
12. Luria, op cit, p 27.
13. Ibid.
14. D Pelham, *The Penguin Book of Kites*, Penguin Books (London), 1976.
15. www.schwinge.co.uk/index.php?id=223.
16. A hydrofoil small water plane area ship; see www.foils.org/.

URBAN
INTERACTIVE

Valentina Croci profiles the work of entertainment design office Area/Code which foregrounds urban locations in its games. As Croci explains the approach of this New York-based partnership, which delivers sat nav-inspired gaming to the mobile phone, demonstrates an inherent understanding of the importance of the physical in enhancing the imaginary.

Valentina Croci

The New York-based entertainment design office Area/Code transforms the urban context into a space of community-centric gaming. Using smart phones or PDAs, users can challenge one another as they move through the streets of the city, partaking in a 'liminal' experience: suspended between the real and the imaginary, between the rules of life and those of a game. Users become 'mutants' as they interpret the role of characters in the dimension of entertainment, while at the same time interacting in the geography of the physical world. This delineates new forms of exploring and using the city. The game thus becomes a fascinating and instantaneously involving tool.

Franz Lantz and Kevin Slavin founded Area/Code in 2005. The two partners have an academic background and have taught at the best New York universities, including Cooper Union, NYU and the Parsons School of Design. Slavin also boasts a professional background with high-profile information and communications technologies companies – IBM, Compaq, Dell, Time/Warner Cable, Microsoft, to mention just a few. Lantz instead has been working for 20 years in the game design field: with gameLab he developed online and downloadable devices, while for POP he designed games for the Cartoon Network, Lifetime TV and VH1. From the beginning both have focused on the use of new technologies, using traditional methods: 'In 2004 we decided that location was the most interesting way to bring the world into our games and to put our games into the world. But the business and technological hurdles in those early days forced us to look elsewhere. So now, our games pull hooks from sharks with GPS transceivers on them, or live television broadcasts, or existing social networks – whatever we can get. The constraints of yesterday's mobile platforms made us look to a landscape that was wider than we had imagined,' explains Slavin.

In fact, when designing systems, Area/Code begin with real-world data, such as GPS positioning systems, Google Map or, in the case of Shark Runners, developed for the Discovery Channel in 2007, transmitters placed on live animals. Here, users competed with sharks, whose real movements were transposed using digital interfaces. The designers are thus using the information produced by the world in which media are 'situated' with respect to specific sites and contexts.

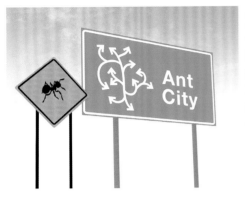

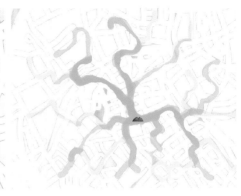

'One of the greatest changes of the last few years,' continues Slavin, 'is the explicit embodiment of player interactions. The Wii has brought the user's body into the game, and GPS has brought his or her location. The EyeToy and the overall field of augmented reality bring the player's immediate environment into the picture. Try doing a Flickr search for "videogame"; you will find images not of screens, but of players. This shift in focus makes clear what videogames are about in the first place: an interaction not with a screen, but with a living system. It was easy to forget this when games were reduced to a controller and a screen. But as we bring the rest of the world into the game (and the game into the world) there is no forgetting that games are really built of rules, emotion and engagement, not pixels and code.'

Design thus passes from the realisation of mere interactive and self-referentially complete products to the production of open systems that interact with real-world variables and players. What is more, the emotional involvement of the user is much more complex and intense with respect to game interactions confined within domestic walls because GPS positioning data are converted into the 'distributed senses' of users acting in real space. This helps to explain games such as Crossroads (2006) and Plundr (2007). The first was developed for two users and employs a cellular GPS system to outline the players' path through city streets. Similar to the famous PacMan, it is necessary to reach a given point while avoiding running into the ghost of Baron Samedi. The second uses WI-FI positioning system (WPS) technology to identify the location of laptop computers in physical space, a position that becomes part of the game. In a sort of private adventure, the user competes with other players in their own locations/games (islands) to capture or exchange goods at the global scale.

In order to create games that involve everyday citizens in the fruition of the city itself, Area/Code was financed by the Knight Foundation, an entity dedicated to education and the role of media in society. In recent years the foundation has had a particular interest in digital supports: 'As the synchronised signals from television fade away and local newspapers disappear, what can we use to produce the necessary sense of community? Community-centric gaming is not a quick solution, but it is part of the evolving set of responses bringing people in proximity back into contact. The Knight Foundation's initiative is an

extraordinarily forward-thinking recognition of the power of play,' Slavin points out. He concludes: 'Beyond these civic concerns, brands are naturally interested in anything that can produce or amplify communities. If these are localised, the benefits are greater to the brand, as well as to the player. In real terms it is easy to imagine games contributing to the overall field of spatial analytics, in which user behaviour can be understood in terms similar to their online activity.'

In a context such as Detroit, a city with a high unemployment level and a partially abandoned centre, a game can become an alternative instrument for using space and a new method for rediscovering an urban reality that offers very little. For example, the ConQwest game platform was used to create real events in 10 American cities. Teams of players equipped with Nokia 6225 cellular phones fitted with photo cameras were asked to visit specific urban areas and photograph signals similar to barcodes to earn points and, as a result, to control the area. An Internet site updated the results of the game, transforming an episode into a spectacular and collective event. The immediacy of involvement this practice enabled may help to develop alternative communities to conventional structures of aggregation – such as sporting or religious events – and, above all, ensure that we are not trapped in 'ghettoes' such as shopping malls.

However, this type of interaction is not without its technical problems. Notwithstanding global access to information, information and telecommunications systems remain highly local because providers must operate under geographic limits. Slavin explains: 'They are not really technical problems as much as business problems. For example, every phone knows exactly where it is, but we cannot get at that data; it is a combination of the obstinate nature of carriers and a few patent problems they got themselves into. The GPS data is open but the carrier data is closed, and closed data environments always create problems.' Furthermore, there are legislative restrictions on the use of these technologies: 'They vary widely on a national level. For example, there is a UK-based company that can pinpoint the location of an anonymous phone with one-metre precision, without anyone downloading anything to their phone, or even being aware of the scan. I believe this is legal now in the US, but there were originally questions about whether this was legal under US "signal intercept" laws.' The question of the lawfulness of device location remains controversial with regard to issues of control and personal privacy, above all when this information is passed on to private entities, for uses beyond those of the game.

At present the iPhone represents the best instrument for location-based gaming because it has excellent software and an integrated

Area/Code, SS+K and Mattia Romeo, ConQwest, 2003–05
The game is a sort of treasure hunt designed by Frank Lantz and SS+K (Kevin Slavin's former company), with Mattia Romeo. It takes place in 10 American cities and was used to promote Qwest Wireless. Students divided into teams according to the schools they attend were given a Nokia 6225 with camera phone. Barcode-like two-dimensional signs (Semacodes), developed by Dennis Crowley, were spread across the city. Players were then asked to intercept and photograph these signs. The images were sent via cellular phone to the central system, where the Semacodes were deciphered to calculate the points accumulated by each team. ConQwest earned wide media coverage and was awarded numerous prizes.

GPS system. What is more, it uses a well-structured system for the distribution of applications through the Apple Store. All the same, in the last five years Area/Code has made use of programmes such as the Skyhooks WPS system that is compatible with other smart phones, or ad hoc platforms developed with Boost Mobile. Even the design of the game interface is restricted by available technology: in the case of Plundr, which functions at the global scale using Google Map, Area/Code needed to adapt the interface to the layout of the aforementioned programmes to ensure the best possible functionality of the game. With Crossroads they were offered more liberty in the design of the visual representation, even though they started with existing topographical maps.

Area/Code's work represents an interdisciplinary possibility related to existing architecture, new media and our everyday habits. Their approach underlines the need to reconsider the instruments of design and, above all, its products, distinguished less as finite objects and more as open systems that imply a complex 'adventure' for the user. Beyond the idea of the game, the involvement of users leads to intangible events, stories and experiences capable of influencing our behaviour or our everyday context. The group's activities highlight the passage from the console in a confined domestic environment to the context of the entire city, transformed into a scenario. This is in line with design trends in the Web 2.0 era, in which digital technology has become the instrument of the unavoidable social necessity of sharing ideas and experiences in blogs and social networks. Game playing is an integral part of this phenomenon and it is thus no accident that Area/Code have also developed a highly successful game together with Facebook. ∆+

Valentina Croci is a freelance journalist of industrial design and architecture. She is also coordinating the Design for Living commission at the Association of Italian Design (ADI). She graduated from Venice University of Architecture (IUAV), and attained an MSc in Architectural History from the Bartlett School of Architecture, University College London. She achieved a PhD in Industrial Design Science at the IUAV with a theoretical thesis on wearable digital technologies.

Area/Code, Plundr, 2007
The first location-based game for PC's, Plundr uses WPS technology and Google Map to identify device positions that are used as part of the game. It is a pirate-like adventure at the global scale in which players arrive by boat on various islands (other user positions), to exchange or steal goods. The game platform is therefore the entire world.

INDIVIDUAL BACKLIST ISSUES OF AD ARE
AVAILABLE FOR PURCHASE AT £22.99/US$45.

TO ORDER AND SUBSCRIBE SEE BELOW

What is Architectural Design?

Founded in 1930, *Architectural Design* (*AD*) is an influential and prestigious publication. It combines the currency and topicality of a newsstand journal with the rigour and production qualities of a book. With an almost unrivalled reputation worldwide, it is consistently at the forefront of cultural thought and design.

Each title of *AD* is edited by an invited guest-editor, who is an international expert in the field. Renowned for being at the leading edge of design and new technologies, *AD* also covers themes as diverse as: architectural history, the environment, interior design, landscape architecture and urban design.

Provocative and inspirational, *AD* inspires theoretical, creative and technological advances. It questions the outcome of technical innovations as well as the far-reaching social, cultural and environmental challenges that present themselves today.

Purchasing Architectural Design

Individual titles of *AD* are sold as books through specialist retailers and flagship bookstores and by online booksellers. It can also be purchased directly from Wiley at www.wiley.com. *AD* can be bought on annual subscription. Special rates are offered for students and individual professionals as well as to institutions.

How to Subscribe

With 6 issues a year, you can subscribe to AD (either print or online), or buy titles individually.

Subscribe today to receive 6 issues delivered direct to your door!

INSTITUTIONAL SUBSCRIPTION
£198 / US$369 combined
print & online

INSTITUTIONAL SUBSCRIPTION
£180 / US$335 print or online

PERSONAL RATE SUBSCRIPTION
£110 / US$170 print only

STUDENT RATE SUBSCRIPTION
£70 / US$110 print only

To subscribe:
Tel: +44 (0) 843 828
Email: cs-journals@wiley.com

Volume 77 No 5
ISBN 978 0470 028377

Volume 77 No 6
ISBN 978 0470 034767

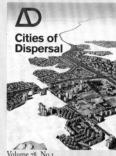

Volume 78 No 1
ISBN 978 0470 066379

Volume 78 No 2
ISBN 978 0470 516874

Volume 78 No 3
ISBN 978 0470 512548

Volume 78 No 4
ISBN 978 0470 519479

Volume 78 No 5
ISBN 978 0470 751220

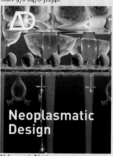

Volume 78 No 6
ISBN 978 0470 519585

Volume 79 No 1
ISBN 978 0470 997796

Volume 79 No 2
ISBN 978 0470 998205

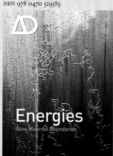

Volume 79 No 3
ISBN 978 0470 753637

Volume 79 No 4
ISBN 978 0470 773000

Volume 79 No 5
ISBN 978 0470 699553

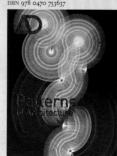

Volume 79 No 6
ISBN 978 0470 699591

Volume 80 No 1
ISBN 978 0470 743195